Don't Sabotage Your Career

11 Power-Filled Steps to Succeed

Best wishes,

Keep on growing
and investing in "you",

Connie

More Praise for *Don't Sabotage Your Career!*

"Regardless of what career stage you are in, 'Don't Sabotage Your Career' is a worthy guide that is crucial for your library. It is loaded with practical tools and resources to help you navigate the workplace by growing your personal and professional life. 'Don't Sabotage Your Career' clearly defines that we must be continually curious and never complacent, in order to improve our career paths and enhance our personal brands."

Diane McDonald

U.S. District Court, District of Idaho; Administrative Office of the U.S. Courts

"This book is a must-have for any young professional! I wish I would have read it 12 years ago when I began in the corporate world...but, better late than never. Thank you, Connie, for this labor of love! I will be purchasing a copy for all new executive hires!"

Nicole Coon

Senior District Manager, Fortune 100 Retailer

"Connie makes it easy to take action that will help you find your passion in your career and advance your skills. This step-by-step guide blends real-world experience from a proven leader and easy-to-follow steps to help navigate your work environment. When you are ready to put your passion and your skills to work in your career, this is the guide for you."

Nora Carpenter

President & CEO, United Way of Treasure Valley

"Few of us ever truly realize our own potential, but Connie gives practical, proven advice on how to unlock those skills and avoid pitfalls that are easily fallen into during our career. Connie's amazing professional attitude has been documented in this book to help others realize their own potential and not unintentionally undermine their own career. I've seen Connie grow throughout her career from a high school graduate to a well-respected and loved CEO by applying the advice she gives in this book. Connie has worked her way to the top and is now sharing her practical and easy-to-follow advice. She's a proven leader who has always led her life with faith, honesty, integrity, and genuine caring about her peers. She has now documented her learnings and offers solid advice about maximizing your career by avoiding self-sabotage traps that can derail it."

Beth Kornegay

Marketing Manager, Kansas City

"Having worked with and for Connie Miller for nearly two decades, I have experienced her leadership and mentorship first hand. She saw my potential even when I did not. Connie's leadership helped me to grow from being a young teller with few career goals, to a respected vice president of an incredible credit union, with a team I am grateful and proud to lead. As I read through 'Don't Sabotage Your Career,' so many memories came flowing back into my mind of the conversations and insights Connie has shared with me over the years. By applying these principles, I have been much more willing to face the difficulties and frustrations that come with any job, and meet any challenge head-on, coming out as a stronger leader in the end. My experiences with Connie's mentorship and leadership are not unique. She has coached and developed many professionals over the years that credit her with a portion of their success. She has spent countless hours helping, mentoring, and coaching individuals inside and outside the credit union to help them reach their full potential. By reading this book and applying the principles Connie shares, you will become a valuable asset to any organization that you are a part of and build a career that you can be proud of. "

Michelle Wall

VP Support Services, Icon Credit Union

Don't Sabotage Your Career

11 Power-Filled Steps to Succeed

CONNIE J. MILLER

ZJN Media & Publishing

Cover illustrated by Paige Weber, Gumption, Copyright © 2008

Author photograph by Pete Grady

FIRST EDITION

Library of Congress ISBN 978-0-692-19556-7

"Keep interested in your own career, however humble; it is a real possession in the changing fortunes of time."

Max Ehrmann, Desiderata

For all the family and friends who have supported and encouraged me, and the many supervisors, employees, and mentors who professionally walked alongside me in our journeys to build our careers and companies. I am humbled and forever grateful that our lives crossed paths, giving me the many shared experiences that inspired me to write this book.

Contents

Introduction and Acknowledgments

My purpose for writing this book is to help you avoid the important pitfalls that can have an unintentional negative impact on your career. This book is written for you if you are a valuable employee who has the talent and desire to build a rich and fulfilling career. It is for you if you strive to make a positive impact at your company, and you want to learn the pitfalls you need to avoid to do so.

I am confident there is something in this book for every person who seeks to scale up and boost their career. This book is intended for those with the true desire to lead and make a positive impact, either through supervision of employees or by leading major initiatives. I include critical insights into how to stop doing the things that likely will prevent you from growing your career, things you might not even be aware of. You will find self-assessments throughout the book to help you build self-awareness, professionalism, and most importantly, a great career – YOUR career.

My passion to write this book rose to the surface when I continued to observe truly gifted and talented employees who were educated and experienced, but simply sabotaged their own selves, often unknowingly and unintentionally. I've seen my peers, employees, and even bosses get caught up in the moment with emotions and the refusal to break away from their own desired personal preferences, which caused them to make grave mistakes that led to distrust and a lack of confidence in them or others. All of this killed their momentum to move their careers forward. Having to take three steps back to rebuild trust or ensure their boss has the confidence that they are in it for the right reasons has hurt them, and the actions were absolutely preventable.

I hope I can shed some light into some of these situations, so you find a way out if this is you, and you don't step into this painful quicksand and not have the ability to get out while building your career or business. I've counseled many employees through this. Those who wish to courageously address their blind spots and take action can win and come out ahead. Those who remain stubborn and self-absorbed to do it entirely their way, regardless of what is best for the company, typically lack the emotional intelligence to see it happening. They forget to stop and assess themselves, their purpose, and the impact that such behavior and emotions has on their team. They put up unintentional road blocks or fail entirely.

I am confident that the insights shared here will propagate beyond your career and into improved personal life and relationships. Even if you have no desire to grow into leadership in your organization, I have included many helpful ways you can create a great culture in your organization and build a fulfilling career. These insights will shore up your personal brand and reputation as well, which follows you from organization to organization. Even if you are self-employed and own your own business with no employees, much of the content is transferable when building relationships and your brand with vendors and clients. It is my belief that the skills shared in this book transform to life outside of work, but they can also hurt you in many walks of life if you fail at them.

Three areas of your life—work, home, and your social circle—always work together. If you are respected as an employee, you are likely respected amongst your friends and family. If you seek to learn and be courageous at work, you will likely be admired in your community and willing to help others. If you are a positive communicator and avoid being a negative drama queen or king, you will become a magnet for healthy people to lean on, and they'll appreciate being in your circle.

I encourage you to think about the insights shared here and use it in both your professional and personal life. These two do impact each other and a change in one area will positively impact a change in the other. For example, if you learn to seek to understand others' views and how they support the company mission at work, you are more likely to use the same skills and tools to build relationships in your personal life. You likely spend an enormous number of hours of your life at work, and the two do meld together. Similar personal characteristics do show up in both places. The two impact each other significantly, such as the personal brand you create for yourself. What you do in your personal life will come into play in building your career, whether you like it or not.

2

It's important to know that every situation in your world is different, and every organization has its own positive attributes and obstacles alike. There are exceptions to every rule, but I do believe the concepts I share in this book will provide tremendous benefit to most situations and career-seeking individuals. The perspective you have towards your situation or employer can often be the most important and impactful, especially if you have obstacles to work through and need to view those obstacles from a different lens than your default personal biases.

More often than not, the solution is right in front of you, ready for you to seize and put it into action, but first you must step back and assess your whole situation fairly. This requires scoping out the landscape from a broad 10,000-foot-level view and caring about the success of your organization with the same care as your personal preferences. Be selfishly unselfish. And let's not forget the importance of courage and determination to reach a good resolution when life hands you an opportunity, often including critical choices and actions to do the right thing for your organization and teams.

I began my professional career after graduating from college with my accounting degree over 35 years ago. I found that I often used the advice contained among the 11 chapters in this book to make a positive impact on moving my career forward along the journey, which earned me challenging and respected roles throughout my career. In my 35 years, although I have worked four positions, I have only worked for three employers, this made possible because of important choices among so many small decisions along the way, all converging into a rich and fulfilling career. There were many forks in the road. I've been able to contribute in such an impactful way towards all of my employers' successes, which in return, continues to contribute daily to my personal and financial success.

My career also required the processing of complex, competitive, and strategic directives that required the ability to adapt to tremendous ongoing change, all while overcoming obstacles. Some were fun, and some were not. Some required simple discipline to stay focused on my professional behavior during emotional and difficult times. Some required deep and personal humility. Others focused on working through nasty situations with a smile. I will share some of these situations in the book. And know there were many situations filled with pure joy while leading people and caring about them as individuals, building their desire to maximize their potential, and believing in them enough to grow and mentor them. Some employees wanted the mentorship, and some did not. My career has included working with many different leadership styles, personalities, and peers in the process. I've worked alongside some top-notch professionals and ever-so-inspiring employees, and also some substantially critical and damaging employees in my organizations. I've seen employees come and go, some who chose to turn to resentment and retaliation to prove themselves or demean others, which never worked in their favor. I've had employees leave my organizations and beg to come back because the grass is not always greener on the other side. Some left and built incredible careers, but most did not.

I will explain the top mistakes employees make, from personal input shared by many of them after their career blunders. I've also seen some employees stick through difficult times, patiently growing in the process, and reach heights they never dreamed of. And then there is the group that settled in the middle, who might have wanted more but weren't willing to put in the effort and take action. Many have found a comfortable niche in their career that suits them in a happy and satisfied career.

After much encouragement from family and friends to get my years of insight and experiences down on paper, I'm excited to share this labor of love with you. I hope it will provide you valuable perspectives to be used at whatever stage you are in your career, and certainly if you are leading others to build theirs.

I have been blessed with an inspiring and fulfilling career, born from a little luck and a lot of choices and hard work. I've made plenty of mistakes, and plenty of great decisions as well. When the time presented itself for each career advancement opportunity, whether it was taking on additional responsibilities or accepting new positions, I was ready and willing, with a dose of courage, education, hands-on experience, and confidence.

My story begins long before college and career. I grew up in a modest household in Boise, Idaho. My mother stayed home to raise my siblings and me while my father worked as a boat mechanic. We lived a simple life in a three-bedroom home with lots of bunkbeds and benches around the kitchen table. We were compelled to do many chores for others to earn the income to purchase what was considered "wants" (such as in-style shoes) as opposed to basic "needs" (such as food), and contribute to the

4

household income. I had many opportunities to do both. These various jobs taught me that if I wanted something, I had to work for it, although I didn't appreciate it at the time.

My mother recently described my childhood behavior as being very "industrious." I also watched my parents be resourceful, something I still value today, inside and outside of work. Although I certainly splurge on occasion, I generally hold a value system that does not include extravagant spending to simply show off that I can. All of these experiences in my childhood helped shape who I am today, even including building up enough courage to never let the rich or mean kids win. I believe that you should never let the obstacles of your past define your future, because those obstacles make you stronger and give you a new appreciation for the depth of what you have inside of you. I was blessed to be fully engulfed in Girl Scouting throughout my childhood. All of this helped form my passion for youth leadership and mentorship throughout my life.

In my teens, I created a smorgasbord of entrepreneurial opportunities to get the things my family couldn't afford. I cleaned houses, was a Tupperware dealer, worked a magazine route, and took on bookkeeping and income tax jobs, not to mention the many babysitting gigs. I dreamt often, but my dreams were really never that big. I wanted to have my own place, find some way to attend college, and buy a car.

I later graduated from Boise State University with a Bachelor's degree in Accountancy. It was a tough four years with my Day-Timer planner hooked to my hip as I juggled an aggressive class schedule with the many jobs required to fund my way through college. My "B" student transcript from high school awarded me no scholarships, so it was all on me then. I made it to graduation with only one small student loan. Although the times and the economy may hold different challenges for you now than for me then, the ingredients for success remain the same.

In addition, I had some great mentors. One of my strongest was Mrs. Kadel, my Girl Scout leader, who helped instill a long-term passion for the goodness of life and people. In a later stage of my life, it was Mr. Wolter, my girlfriend's father, who early on made me promise that before I could drop out of college, I had to go talk to him first. Prophetically, that day did come. I was juggling a heavy class load and several part-time jobs, and I was ready to drop out from sheer exhaustion and discouragement. I decided to quit school, but I honored my promise and went to talk to Mr. Wolter before making it official. Needless to say, after that tough and uncomfortable conversation, I was back in class the next day. I am so grateful now to have had a little persuasive tough love then, and someone with more experience to remind me that my potential was great, and the present pain was only temporary.

I share this experience to illustrate the importance of having strong accountability partners in building your career. Everyone needs them. Find quality ones who will tell you what you *need* to hear (as opposed to what you *want* to hear) and have your long-term best interest at heart, not your short-term friendship.

Enjoy this book! I hope you find many key takeaways that you can use in each difficult situation you face. It is likely a few of the 11 chapters can be applied to each situation you face to give you the breakthrough you need to build your career. Remember that change requires muscle memory to stick. Practice is required—sheer willpower is not enough, although it is a great foundation. So take some of the following concepts and put processes in place to get the change to stick if an area resonates with you.

I would be remiss if I didn't mention that the content in this book comes primarily from many inspiring employees I have worked with over the years, as well as some respected bosses and professionals who have walked alongside me in my journey. Each found a way to reach a new step on their career ladder and lead others to do the same. Their success is the result of the choices they made that made a big impact on the level of respect and influence they earned. These employees and friends showed the courage to stand proudly for the company they work for and often chose well during difficult moments of truth. Others found a way to pull courage from deep within and use it when they least wanted to, but knew it was the best thing for the good of the organization. I've had to do both. In addition, observing the damage others caused to their careers when they took the wrong fork in the road taught me many lessons over the years. I am an observer and use what I observe often.

I want to thank my husband, Neil, who celebrated much success with me throughout the years, and stood by me through the occasional trials. He's been my rock as I processed many situations, and his wisdom was usually right on. He has supported me when the job duties called, and has always been an encourager to hold true to doing the right thing. I seldom bring home my work-related issues, but when I needed to sort something big out, he's always been there with some great insight and guidance. His wisdom is unwavering.

Also, I have much love and appreciation for my three boys, Zachary, Jacob, and Nathaniel, as they supported me when I juggled their many activities through the jungle of obligations and meetings. They allowed me to experience the fulfillment gained from my career with many tradeoffs, while also showing me the joy of being a mom. I love them with my whole being. I was fortunate to have employers who always supported the flexibility to be with my family during their special life events and needs.

I would be remiss if I also didn't thank two specific incredible bosses from early in my career, Luanne Crump and David Berent, who both taught me so much about never losing sight of who one serves in your organizations, the members and customers. Both were willing to supportively and honestly tell me what I needed to hear to grow and develop my career. And both appreciated the value I brought with many of the concepts I share in this book. I can also say the same about the supportive Board of Directors I have worked with throughout the years. I appreciate their patience and positive influence while building my career, a successful one I will always treasure and now share with you.

Connie J. Miller
President and CEO, Icon Credit Union

1: Only YOU Can Own Your Career

Having a job is very different than owning your own career.

If you find yourself caring more about what your moment-to-moment life is like at work and how you feel today, how you like the people you work with, and if the job entails your favorite tasks or responsibilities of the day, it's likely you see your work as "just a job." If you find you have the short-sighted need to "love" your job each and every day, instead of finding it in you to invest in yourself to gain new skills for a future opportunity, you likely see your purpose of employment being anything but building your career. It's important to ask yourself if you care more about how you feel in the moment when at work, rather than how your current job can be a means to gain new skills to scale up your working life experience, leading to what is called a career. A career is going to bring you exponentially greater wages, benefits, satisfaction, and personal growth. If you find it easy to jump ship tomorrow and change jobs if you don't like what today brings, you run the risk of sabotaging your career, or not even having one. This is because your vision of (and consequently commitment to) your future is unclear.

If you want to call your job a career, you need to look at your present-day work as an investment to get you greater value down the road. You can't be a routine job hopper and expect to grow a worthy career.

Just understanding the difference between a job and a career will bring you one step closer to creating and owning whatever that career looks like to you. It's important to ask yourself what you value more: owning your career for future success or working just hard enough to get enough money to last until the next payday.

Make a list of why you go to work each day, and separate the items into the two approaches, job or career, and think about how they are different. One may be no better in how you achieve happiness in the short-term. But building a career is truly building an investment in your future, which reaps many rewards long term.

Careers can bring job stability, increased wages and benefits, improved life experiences and opportunities, and the fulfillment that you earned the responsibility to be entrusted to build others' personal growth and careers. Creating a career simply reaps significantly more benefits than just working in one job after another.

Owning your own career takes much more effort and commitment than simply holding a good job. The career approach transforms a job into an experience where you can learn and grow new skills, gain and appreciate a greater tolerance for differences, build something bigger than you, increase security through job stability, increase finances for a more enjoyable life and flexibility down the road, and lastly, what I love most is that it gives you the earned respect within your company.

Often, I am asked what one thing attributed to the success in my career, eventually being blessed and selected to be the President and CEO of a unique and successful institution with $290 million in assets today. At the top of the list is the principle of *owning* my own career. And I mean truly owning it at all levels, starting over 35 years ago. It has been just me, myself, and I that held the responsibility of seizing the opportunities that arose, even with the incredible bosses that encouraged me along the way. They didn't own my career, I did. It wasn't their responsibility to own my career, it was mine. I never had the benefit of slipping into positions because of sheer luck, a family business, or close acquaintances that helped get me that next promotion. I had to make my own luck. Each step along the way was mastered through a committed work ethic, focusing on mastering success in each area of my job description, exhibiting professionalism during stressful situations, and building expertise along the way. To start, one of the most committed actions in the beginning started with completing my accounting degree, a requirement that landed me that first career accounting job to get the ball rolling.

Simply said, don't be complacent in the moment and take too many shortcuts. Stay focused on a realistic long-term view of why you need to put in the extra effort. Don't let someone else learn more than you because you are just not in the mood or unsure if it will matter. In time, it *all* matters. And don't give up when it gets hard.

Let's get started! To ensure you are owning the next step to advance your career, take this quick assessment:

Quick Sabotage Assessment: How are you owning your own career?

CAREER BUILDING CHARACTERISTICS	Y/N	CAREER SABOTAGING CHARACTERISTICS	Y/N
Am I performing standard expectations well in my current position before I expect my employer to promote me to a new position?		*Do I routinely expect that I should be considered for the next job opportunity, even if I am not performing at high standards in my current role?*	
Do I know my job responsibilities? Have I assessed the areas I still need to gain expertise and training?		*Do I passively take each day as it comes, expecting that if my boss wants me to do something, they will ask?*	
Do I ask questions while learning my job if I don't understand? Do I take notes, so I can refer back to them if needed?		*Do I accept that if I forget something during training, I can just interrupt my boss or coworker and ask them to train me again, before I try to find the answer first?*	
Do I ask for written procedures and policies so I can refer to them as needed? If I see corrections that need to be made, do I share recommendations to improve them and ensure they are current?		*Do I rely solely on my memory and know if I make a mistake, someone will remind me what to do or what the procedure says?*	
Do I share with my boss my career goals?		*Do I expect my boss to tell me if they want me to apply for the next opportunity?*	

(Quick Sabotage Assessment, Cont.)

CAREER BUILDING CHARACTERISTICS	Y/N	CAREER SABOTAGING CHARACTERISTICS	Y/N
Do I study hard in areas that I know will help me perform my job better? Even if it doesn't come easily to me?		*Do I avoid studying what I don't know but am expected to know?*	
Do I inquire what training or education I might need to be qualified for the next advancement in my company? Do I look at minimum qualifications today so I am better prepared for the next potential level of advancement when it happens?		*Do I expect that my boss will tell me what they require for the next logical position to be promoted to? Do I wait until a position becomes available and then ask what the requirements are?*	
Do I ask questions of other departments to understand how their work affects my job responsibilities and department, in order to understand a broader perspective?		*Do I stay quiet in staff meetings and discussions if the topics are not related to my immediate job responsibilities? Do I tune out conversations that don't apply to my immediate job?*	
Do I take the time to think how I can use my knowledge to help others or improve the process, and then offer to help where needed?		*Do I stay solely focused on my own job responsibilities, and do I get complacent so long as I'm doing my duties to my own satisfaction?*	
Do I ask to job shadow other positions I may be interested in to determine if the other positions might be of interest to me down the road?		*Do I ask for a job advancement when I'm not quite sure I'd even enjoy the job, but I pursue it anyway because it pays more or I like the title?*	
Am I proactive and considered a hard worker?		*Am I nonchalant or lazy?*	

In addition to the many areas discussed in this book, a significant initial step to build your career is to stay focused on mastering your current job first. Go-getters are often more emotionally invested in the next opportunity and building their career than becoming the expert in their current position, although they never lose sight of being the knowledgeable employee. Each time you perfect your current job role, you are more prepared for the next job and will perform there at a greater performance level when you get promoted. I'll expand on this more in a few of the chapters in this book, but simply stated, master your current job first before you become distracted about the next job. You will not do yourself any favors if you are an underperformer today in your current job and begging for a different job. It is more difficult for you to get the next promotion if you are substandard in your current role, regardless of the reason. You will sabotage yourself if you start whining about why a coworker who is more skilled overall got the most recent promotion, or pushing your supervisor to promote you when you aren't meeting your current goals, for example.

But there are other factors as I settled into my many jobs over the years. I can recall many times where I took the initiative to learn the world around my immediate circle of responsibilities and influence. It simply was about expanding my horizons to include a deeper layer than my immediate responsibilities. I never forgot to attend to this, while simultaneously never losing sight that my primary obligation was to my existing job responsibilities. I made sure I received glowing performance evaluations and perfected the areas of weakness, and alongside that I was always learning about the next job responsibility or opportunity on the horizon.

Early in my career, I worked as an accountant at the Girl Scouts. I was young and shy. My day-to-day responsibilities included balancing general ledger accounts and preparing financial statements. Without being asked, I expanded my curiosity into learning about the other departments, the organization as a whole, and how all the parts worked together. The ledgers and financial statements were not an end to themselves—they *meant* something. They described *actual people* doing *actual things* that made the world a better place.

I looked for opportunities to provide beneficial analytical information that would help other departments. For example, while assessing donor relations and contributions for the fund development department, I expanded my explorations to include learning more about the fund development process itself, and how that was tracked. I also studied how the product sales department and their cookie program worked, so I could provide additional analysis broken down by troops and girls that helped determine which areas may be in need of a higher level of support from the council for higher product sales success, which in turn helped the council and each girl in those areas. I studied the entrepreneurial skills girls learned from cookie sales. Even though the tasks and goals within those departments were not in my job description, I listened intently in meetings to learn about their business model and how I might be able to provide data or reports to help them become more successful and informed. During this process, I learned about campers' needs at summer camps, the routes of the semi-trucks delivering cookies, and the retail store inventory process. I attended volunteer events and learned firsthand from the volunteers what their needs were while serving girls more effectively.

Every bit of new information I learned in my accountant role added value, making me more valuable to the organization in many ways. No one asked me to stretch in these areas. But I knew if I continuously expanded my knowledge about the company, I would understand their mission and be able to support them more effectively. Now, to be honest, I didn't know how that would eventually impact my career in the moment, but looking back, it set the stage for my next opportunity in my career. I truly cannot remember ever being more focused on the next promotion than my current job. My promotions just happened because I was more obsessed about performing with excellence in each of my current positions and always learning a little more outside the circle of my current roles. That alone prepared me for the next opportunity, and an incredibly satisfying career. An added bonus was that others saw me as a superstar and company advocate, leading to many accolades in the process, boosting my confidence and courage.

When I became the VP of Finance at Idahy Federal Credit Union (now known as Icon Credit Union), I was privileged to be a part of the leadership team and participate in many strategic discussions that were centered on other departments' roles. My Girl Scout experience was a ready foundation to get started. I was fairly new to the credit union industry, so I knew I had much to learn. I was vigilant about learning the one layer of business beyond my own department's responsibilities, so I could better serve the entire company.

I was blessed when I started working at Idahy, because my first large initiative was building a large Y2K contingency plan for every system in the company. (Y2K was the "Year 2000" computer glitch that at the time was threatening to shut down the internet, the power grid, and possibly the entire economy. Some were very concerned.) The project included comprehensive testing and documentation of every computer system to ensure that if there was a power outage or system glitch in one integrated system, a quick backup plan was ready to launch. Understand that up to that point, my experience was primarily accounting and finance related. But now I was also responsible for supervising the technology area. I knew it was going to be a challenge, but one I was up to taking on. My boss reassured me he would teach me the ropes to master the job, and he lived up to that promise.

What that major initiative allowed me to do was research systems in other departments and identify a backup recovery process for each department. I embraced this project as an opportunity to learn as much as I could about the entire company and industry. To create a backup plan for loan document printing, for example, required me to learn how loans were processed, which was not something in my immediate area of finance knowledge or responsibility. When I became the CEO ten years later, that investment in focused learning over the prior years as the VP of Finance was a huge asset to me in leading the entire organization later on. Not only was it the technical and business knowledge that was beneficial, but the relationships I developed during that experience ended up becoming some of my greatest allies.

You might not have that tremendous opportunity that I had with building a company-wide contingency plan in order to be involved in other departments when you start a new job or enter a new department. However, you do have the opportunity to ask questions beyond your own day-to-day tasks that you might not think about. Problems are everywhere waiting for that one person (you, for example) to solve them. Volunteering to serve on the staff picnic committee or Christmas party committee gives you instant exposure to employees from other departments, a perfect time to learn about their departments and a few things they might do in their day-to-day jobs, which leads to a great opportunity to inquire more. When you share space in the company breakroom, it's a golden time to inquire about other's work. Use your coaching sessions with your boss to learn one new thing each time you meet. Inquire often about the strategic direction of the company, and regularly ask your boss what the next new thing would be for you to learn to help the organization. Look for things you can help your boss with and take off their plate. The internet is full of wisdom and learning material. Spending just 15 minutes each day reading an article from a local trade association, for example, will provide tremendous new insight that will elevate you above your peers as you grow your expertise at a new level. Commit to being continuously curious. Never become complacent or too comfortable, unless that's just where you want your career to stay. Far more employees sit and wait for the leadership to tell them what to learn next. Don't be "that employee."

Once you feel you have mastered your current position to a level where your performance is exceeding expectations, the time is ripe to begin expanding your knowledge base. The best time to learn about a new position in the organization you have your eye on is before the job ever becomes available. Be observant as to what the next position for you might be to advance your career, and then find opportunities to learn that position *today*. If you have downtime, for example, use that time wisely to study the job description of the position you are intrigued by. Create a list of how you can learn bits and pieces of that job, and study related procedures, for example. Talk to your boss to see if there are job shadow opportunities to keep you educated and informed. This will help you identify if it is really a job you would thrive in and enjoy. Depending on the size of the company, this may take some creative scheduling and sacrifice on your part, and donating extra time without pay. Study your competition and how you might create a differentiator. Ask about education or certifications you can start working on today, even though they might not be needed in your current role.

I remember a conversation I had with my boss, David Berent, a few years into my job as VP of Finance at Idahy, where we discussed a three-year graduate level credit union management program, and the likely need for that certification for my resume if I ever wanted to become a CEO. At that time, I didn't know if the CEO role was anything I would want in the future, but I knew it could only help me in my current role. Even though going back to school wasn't something I desired or wanted to invest in, as my husband and I were still raising three active young boys, I knew *if my boss was discussing this with me, I should take that as a supportive hint*. With a little encouragement, I jumped in, and was so glad I did. What I learned in that program helped prepare me immensely in my new CEO role a few years later, and it also helped me immensely in my current position at that time as VP of Finance.

Know that it doesn't have to be a big decision like a three-year graduate level course that you invest in. It can be investments in much smaller action steps. If you are a receptionist, for example, request more information about your company's pricing strategies, vendor management, or inventory control. If you are a teller at a financial institution, ask to study how loans are underwritten or how new accounts are processed in your downtime when a customer is not immediately present to serve. Spending your downtime doing this instead of chatting with the coworker next to you will become more beneficial in building your career. If you are a server at a restaurant, learn how scheduling works with staffing or what ordering requirements are for food inventory management. Every job has something you can learn more about. Think immediately about your boss and how you can take the load off of their plate and help them out.

Owning your career also includes owning how to overcome obstacles when you get stuck. You won't know everything and you will need help with how to understand or complete a more complex task on occasion. As you learn and grow within your career, you will run into tougher obstacles and new territories where you have no previous experience or existing knowledge (at least you *should* if you are truly challenging yourself and striving for growth).

So what do you do when you run into obstacles where you simply aren't sure how to do a particular task or are asked a question you've never been asked before? If it is part of your current job description or expected duties, know it is your responsibility to perform and learn, even though you might not currently have the knowledge, or the procedures are unclear. Take the bull by the horns, as they say, and create an action plan to build your knowledge. That might include scheduling a training already offered online, attending a new course, or scheduling time with another employee who knows how to do the work. And sometimes, you just need to study on personal time to get it accomplished. The most important thing to recognize is that you own the responsibility for your preparation requirements to do the job or learn a new role. Don't wait for your company to take the first step to get you trained!

Occasionally, I will hear an employee share that the reason they are not performing is because they weren't properly trained. Ugh! My question is what did you do to proactively request your needed training? You usually know what knowledge you aren't completely confident with, and you should know that better than your employer does. What do you do to ensure you are equipped and prepared to complete your job well? If you don't know how to do something, seek first and then ask. Don't wait for your boss to ask why you aren't doing something. As you grow your career, you must get even more proactive at asking in order to receive expertise, training, and education. After all, becoming a leader in your company will deal you many challenges where you must proactively solve a problem by stepping into it and finding solutions. You must be able to learn how to do this without your boss's prodding. Keep the communication open with your boss, and always discuss priorities with them in your work flow so you are both on the same page.

If the opportunity for you to grow your knowledge and skills does not exist in your own company, first take a step back and ask if you are being honest about this with yourself. Is there an area you have not stepped into that could change this perception of you or your boss? It might be an area you simply don't like, but could be a worthy investment for you. If you discover there truly is no opportunity, you cannot grow your career by staying in a dead-end position. You must ask yourself if you are ready to take the next step.

After 12 years at my first job working as an accountant, I did get to a stage where I knew I had learned everything possible and it was time to step out of my comfort zone and into new territory. I had provided them everything possible that I had to offer. I was terrified, but also excited about what that next job might look like for me. I knew it would require me to learn new things, a lot of new things! So I stepped out and started interviewing, something I hadn't done in 12 years. I landed in a wholesale credit union where most everything I touched was new, and I embraced it as growing the next level in my career. It worked masterfully.

But I caution you, don't move out of your organization if the opportunity is on the horizon, but just not yet available today. Waiting might be better than starting over. Give your company the time to grow to use your skills, because you'll enter that new role with a solid foundation of knowledge within the same company.

Please note that not all employees desire to grow in a company because they don't wish to assume the expanded responsibilities, stress, travel, or supervisory duties. Not everyone is cut out to be a supervisor, for example.

It is commendable if you recognize you are not ready for the next step and simply enjoy your current position, perform it well and with a strong work ethic, and be a positive team player in the process. Every company needs a certain number of what I've heard referred to as "Steady Eddies." Know it is okay if you are comfortable in your position and want to remain in it for several years or retire from it down the road, as long as it fits with your company's needs, but also be fair with your expectations of increased pay if this is where you are at. You cannot stay comfortable in the same position and also expect your company to treat your compensation package as if you took on a new, more complex role in the company just because you increased your longevity. I call this a "keep the seat warm" type of position choice, and every company needs a few of these valuable employees who are okay in their current positions and consistently provide value to their employer.

The benefits are typically less stress and a higher comfort level, and those are benefits worthwhile to certain individuals. These individuals are not likely trying to build their career, but more enjoying their career as a satisfying and comfortable one with steady and unchanged job responsibilities. If this is you, it is not a bad thing. It is simply important you are aware of your choices and fair with the expectations of your company on your compensation package. It is likely one where your compensation will remain unchanged except a cost of living increase on occasion. Know that many chapters in this book will still apply to you if you have accepted this situation and status in your career. Most of it still applies in order to prevent doing something that will damage your current position or how you are perceived in your organization.

Finally, take your job performance seriously—not only your version of the job, but the version your boss actually evaluates you on. We all have blind spots, and you will too. Do some serious self-assessment thinking after every performance review in how you can perform better. It is human nature that we tend to focus on the few areas of weakness or opportunities for growth after a performance review and think our boss isn't seeing all the great work we do.

Owning it is the first step. Own and continue building the strengths you have and where you are performing well. Own even more your areas of opportunities discussed and fiercely grow them quickly and professionally. Ask for feedback often to ensure you are on the right track and that you interpreted the feedback you received correctly. Listen and ask questions so you fully understand what your boss is looking for. Go into this process without resentment or taking things personally, or it will cause you to be negative along the way. No one likes criticism, and no one likes to develop employees who are defensive. But humility and humbleness are virtues that will carry you a long way in building your career. Leave your self-serving ego at the door. Better yet, leave it under the mat at home. Use pride wisely. And remember, torturing or tormenting your boss along the way when they were only trying to help you build your career is a very bad plan. No one enjoys delivering constructive criticism, so take it with open arms and as a gift from the messenger, so they'll be more willing to deliver you some great suggestions in the future. Who knows? Your boss today might be your employee tomorrow! Wouldn't it be nice to have mutual respect and an excellent professional understanding?

Even as a President and CEO, I have had times where I have utilized a CEO executive coach and completed a 360-degree self-assessment and evaluation process to identify my own personal blind spots. I am not perfect and must grow as well. We all do. For example, I learned recently that my ability to have expertise and hold most of the answers was stifling the growth in my team, so I learned I needed to shift to ask more guiding questions and provide less advice. I had previously thought my actions were helpful when they were, in fact, not helpful at times. This was something critically good to learn, but I may not have been able to learn this at the depth needed without the willingness to assess the situation and to accept candid feedback. Be humble and always be willing to grow, regardless of the level you are in within your organization. We all have areas that will need polished on occasion as our organizations change and become more complex, as our teams change, and as our competitive advantage continues to be challenged.

I have a plaque in my office that sums this chapter up, and it reads, *"Life is not about finding yourself. Life is about creating yourself."* You have amazing power to create the "you" in your career to build the career you want.

2: Don't Sabotage Your Personal Brand

At every stage in your career, it is important that you are vigilant about building a personal brand that an employer would be proud to put on the front cover of the paper or their annual report. Your brand follows you to every job in your journey, and this is now truer than ever with the prevalence of social media. Never discount the value of your reputation, both professionally and while off the clock. Work hard to continue to build it to be commendable and one of integrity and consistency.

You can do everything right with building your education and technical expertise for advancement, but if your personal brand stinks, your career will hit a roadblock. Become the person everyone wants on their team, not the person that gives your coworkers or supervisor anxiety because of how you might likely respond or behave. Here is a quick assessment to determine how strong your brand is and a look at what behaviors you may have to change in order to improve your reputation.

Quick Sabotage Assessment: Do I consistently build a strong personal brand for myself?

CAREER BUILDING CHARACTERISTICS	Y/N	CAREER SABOTAGING CHARACTERISTICS	Y/N
Do I strive to work with integrity in every decision?		*Do I push the limits to gain a sale or cheat on my expense report?*	
Do I find ways to communicate openly and fairly?		*Do I shy away from speaking truth into a conversation, but then vent at a later time to someone else?*	

(Quick Sabotage Assessment, Cont.)

CAREER BUILDING CHARACTERISTICS	Y/N	CAREER SABOTAGING CHARACTERISTICS	Y/N
Do I avoid destroying another person's reputation and brand through gossip?		Do I gossip and create drama?	
Do I finish the job as expected and promised?		Do I take shortcuts because I can get away with it and because the boss will never know?	
Do I present myself on social media as genuine and accepting of others? Do others see me as inclusive?		Do I attack the differences of opinions in a judgmental and unforgiving manner?	
Do I support the mission and values of my organization in all of my affairs?		Do I share that I don't believe in things my employer stands for? Do I publicly share my personal irritants about my employer, hurting their brand?	
Do I fulfill my commitments when I volunteer for a board or volunteer activity?		Do I shun my duties and not live up to my agreed-upon commitments? Do I show up to my board meetings unprepared? Do I accept appointments only to look good on my resume?	
Do I clean up after myself?		Do I leave the grocery cart in the parking lot or my dishes in the breakroom sink, knowing someone else will put them away or wash them?	
Do I meet deadlines as promised?		Do I create a crisis for others because of my lack of time management?	

(Quick Sabotage Assessment, Cont.)

CAREER BUILDING CHARACTERISTICS	Y/N	CAREER SABOTAGING CHARACTERISTICS	Y/N
Do I take responsibility for my own actions? Am I accountable to my team and own my part? Do I ask for help as soon as I need help or when things become unclear?		*Do I play the victim card and blame my boss or others in the company when I didn't perform and meet expectations? Do I wait for my company to come forward and explain when I don't understand? Do I blame my situation on what others have done to me as to why I behave in an undesirable manner?*	
Do I stand tall when an enemy falsely accuses me and focus only on my role and what I can control?		*Do I retaliate and attempt to destroy others?*	
Do I use professional language?		*Do I swear or use inappropriate words? Do I use anger and outbursts to get attention?*	
Do I stay focused on working while I am at work?		*Am I distracted by cell phone or internet browsing while on company time? Do I waste time chatting with coworkers when it is not break time?*	

Whether you recognize it or not, you are always in a job interview, at least figuratively. Those around you observe how you communicate, what your belief system is, and mostly how you make them feel. It doesn't matter if you are an extrovert or an introvert; you build your brand by being responsible, kind, compassionate, honest, and empathetic. Sometimes I will hear, "I'm just not a touchy feely type of person." That's okay, but you can still be warm and kind in the moment, while also being encouraging through showing appreciation and acceptance. Here's some helpful insight that is important to building your reputation and brand. Remember, no two people have the same brand, but many have created a dependable one that others would love to have on their team. Know if you are a jerk, the word spreads fast. Also, if you have a stellar reputation, your name also comes up in conversations when others are looking for like-minded people to associate with.

Live and work with integrity.

Simply said, be a good person, both legally (following the rules) and ethically (following the spirit of the rules). One of my favorite quotes I heard years ago is, *"Do the right thing, even when no one is looking."* Hopefully you have a good conscience that simply reminds you what is right and wrong. Your conscience should be tapping you on the shoulder on occasion to wake you up. In that moment, do the gut check and ask if this decision was presented in a job interview or on Facebook, would it make you proud? Would it make your employer, friends, and family proud to have you in their circle? Would they want to give you a job reference if you asked, based on what they know or observed about you? Would it make your community proud? Is your time with your "friends" equally about creating a good brand, or is it more about having fun that puts your professional reputation at risk? I used to tell my children, "Be careful about having short-term fun that may create long-term pain." The same is true of our actions as adults in building our brand. Your brand is a long-term investment and hard to correct quickly when damaged.

There is no substitute for being known as a great human being. Just today (and I am not kidding about this), I was privy to a call looking for my son, Jacob, who was unavailable. It was Jacob's boss on the other line, and when I mentioned who I was and that I could give him a message, his boss replied, "No, that's okay. I wanted to tell him what a great job he did on a video. But, you need to know we love Jacob. He's a great worker, but more importantly, he's an incredibly good human being." It is cosmic that this call came in today as I was writing this chapter, but it solidified how important it is to be known as a good person. I can assure you that the life choices resulting in that single compliment will guarantee Jacob a promotion if one becomes available in the future, even if his skillset or education might not be exactly what they are looking for. Employers will often take a chance to get good character on their teams. An employer can train job skills, but only the employee can bring good character to the job.

Learn to avoid drama and sharpen your conflict resolution skills.

For those who know me well, they know drama is my single biggest personal pet peeve. I hate it! I attempt to steer clear of it and certainly don't tolerate it well. Drama is created in the workplace because employees want to shun their accountability at work or in life or are overly critical of personal attributes or accountability in others. Typically, employees that create drama and become negative gossipers are unable to have difficult and crucial conversations. What most people don't realize is healthy conflict and problem resolution meetings bring tremendous benefit and usually end with a positive outcome if done with the right intent. Drama and gossip can destroy teams and create a distraction like no other. Drama tarnishes your brand, and can even kill it. Those who choose to participate or get sucked into it make poor decisions in their career, and even worse, rob themselves of joy and happiness in the moment. Employees make horrible supervisors if they allow drama and refuse to draw a line in the sand regarding it. Drama and gossip are a form of fierce manipulation delivered in an often-hidden disguise by those who choose to be victims. Chapter Four is entirely devoted to the subject of drama and conflict, because it is a career killer if you can't gain control of it, and a huge epidemic as people rely on technology to communicate more than ever before.

Continue learning. Learn enough so you can do it right the first time. Learn enough to earn more responsibility and be ready for the next promotion.

As you grow your career, each task you complete adds or takes away one layer of your brand and reputation in the workplace, good or bad. If you do a quality job as trained and directed, it is appreciated and noticed. If you leave the job unfinished, take shortcuts, or leave tasks for someone else to finish, it has a negative effect. This is true of the most basic responsibilities.

Let's assume for a minute that you let the phone ring a few extra times because you know your coworker will pick it up. You simply chose to take a shortcut to do less. Make no mistake—others notice. They might not be telling you they notice, but they do. Never discount the power of silent observation by those around you. The simplest of tasks left for someone else to finish creates a negative brand for you that might include something like lazy, distracted, disengaged, or self-centered. Is that the brand that will get you promoted, or engender others to buy in to your future leadership?

Not likely. However, if you instead create a personal goal that you will answer as many calls as you can, while serving the customer well, the boss and those around you will notice. And here's the great thing about the latter example: If you are promoted someday in the future to a supervisor role, you will start your leadership position off on a good start with immediate respect from your team. It will make sense to them why you got the promotion. But if you were the slacker and somehow managed to get promoted, you might have landed the job, but you will start your new leadership role off with less respect, fewer followers, and probably even the passive sabotage that you yourself once engaged in. Which would you rather have?

Don't wait for someone to give you more responsibility. Ask for it, and then listen carefully for the reasons if your request is denied. Oftentimes, it may be only a temporary circumstance, such as current workload or a staff shortage, but assess it anyway regarding the possibility of change in the near future. Be open to the discussion and add value to the solution with what your part may be in earning more responsibility.

Be honest with your own self-assessment of your performance. Are you truly ready? Be careful though and never ask for more responsibilities if you aren't performing your current job well. Nail that one down first, and then ask for more. The first consideration a boss will give when you ask for more responsibility is if you are performing well in your current position. Be reasonable with the length of time you have been performing your current position and if you have truly mastered it, rather than ask just because you want more money or want to work in a different environment.

Jumping into more responsibility before you are truly ready can become a quick obstacle in building your career and can actually set you back. For example, if you are a receptionist and learning the product and services for the company by fielding service calls, and you ask to be promoted to a sales representative so you may earn more money, ask yourself if spending another six months in the receptionist role to fully understand all the features of the products could give you a great head start in your success as a sales representative. It is always a good idea to discuss with your supervisor your aspirations and create a game plan for development in order to be ready when the opportunity finally arrives. I recommend one-year intervals as a general guide before you ask for the next promotion.

This allows you to master your current job to perfection, something that adds incredible value to your brand.

Getting ready for a promotion should occur long before the position you desire actually opens up. Identify what skills and expertise you may need to be ready. Visit with the person who does that job today and learn where your gaps might be. Don't be bashful about taking your career growth into your own hands. And be honest with yourself regarding your comfortableness with managing people or stepping into a job that you may not be successful at or enjoy. Sometimes I see employees who are thriving in a current job request a move for the wrong reasons, and then become a substandard employee, which causes them unnecessary stress and also hurts their career. Ask for feedback from your boss and truly listen without becoming defensive. Take their feedback as an action plan to improve, instead of as personal criticism. Hopefully they will give it to you and help build your plan. Even if the feedback sounds like personal criticism, still listen for a message of what improvements you should make, even if the messenger is unpleasant.

And finally, find a good mentor you trust and seek honest advice from them. Some of the best insight I received in my career was from mentors, *but only after I asked for it.* No one likes to give constructive criticism, but if you ask for it, it makes it easier to deliver and worth its weight in gold. Listen carefully, as mentors often see an expanded view, more than you might see, and provide nonthreatening and invaluable insight. Meet with them and ask questions such as the following:

- What do you think my greatest strengths are in my current role?
- What do you consider my natural talents that I could work to improve?
- If I wanted to grow my career, what one thing would you recommend I do?
- Is there someone I should meet with to explore what steps I can take to further develop my career?

Get the advice. Then *act on it.* Sometimes all you need to do is take a class or complete some job-sharing activities. Other times, you may need to make a large investment and commit to a much larger plan, such as completing a higher level of education or a certification. Know what that is and invest in yourself, and never approach it as just doing it to make your company happy. Learn and grow from the process, as no one can ever take that away from you, wherever you go.

Again, it's important you don't seek advice and then fail to act on it, especially if the advice comes from your current employer. I have had insightful and valuable career development conversations with employees in the past, only to find after several months that they haven't taken any action on what we discussed. They wanted to move up and earn more money, they sought solid advice, but then they didn't act on that advice. This sends the strong message that they want a quick fix but don't want to do the work.

If you ask for advice, create a plan and be ready to act in some capacity to build your career. Just expressing what you want is not sufficient to grow your career, and it can be frustrating to employers if you aren't doing your part. It's often said that the difference between successful and unsuccessful people is simply that successful people get it done.

Some career development plans take months to complete, so don't procrastinate until you sense an opening might be coming up soon. I remember a time several years ago when I had discussed with my CEO regarding whether he felt I needed a certain industry specific three-year graduate level course if I ever wanted to become a CEO, and he recommended it. Although I knew of no openings, and had no idea when that opportunity might ultimately arise, I pursued and completed the course because the thought of becoming a CEO was something on my possibilities list, even though I didn't know yet if it would be right for me, or even in the cards for what I would be qualified to do or even want. Getting training for a potential opportunity is one way of finding out if that's something you'd ultimately like to do.

That training was so hard. I had to relearn how to memorize, and used my fallback flash cards from many years ago to get through it. Years later, a CEO opportunity presented itself and it helped tremendously that I had pursued this training. It would have been too late to attempt getting that course completed when the opportunity for the CEO position presented itself, and it was a decision that was invaluable in providing additional expertise I did not have at the time, but have used today.

In pursuing that extra training, I enhanced my personal brand to include the fact that I will do whatever it takes to be prepared to be a qualified CEO. If

I had not pursued that certification, I'm guessing my brand would have been less desirable.

Learning also comes in the form of asking a lot of questions and being naturally curious about expanding your horizons and knowledge base. Don't be afraid to seek to understand what you work with, digging one layer deeper. It will help you understand more about what you do in your current job responsibilities and prepare you for more responsibilities. If you are in team meetings, for example, inquire about the details or the "why" with agenda topics that may not be in your current roles and responsibilities realm, but will provide new education for you. Take the time to understand how something works. I often took the time in my career to listen carefully to the details being discussed, and it allowed me to gain a stronger well-rounded knowledge base, preparing me for broader responsibilities later on.

A final comment I would make with building your brand with learning is that expertise and education by themselves are not enough. It is difficult to promote an employee who does not have good work ethic, is a poor team player, or has a bad attitude. So assess all the intangibles in your personality that frequently carry more weight than your longevity or technical expertise when hiring or promoting employees. Never expect that your longevity in the company or education level gives you the right to the next promotion. Remember that some jobs are just not meant for you and your personality. Even more importantly, leadership opportunities require good role models who have built a trusted brand.

It's just as important to be professional outside of work, not just while in the building or on the clock.

It is important to remember that what you do outside of your day job builds your brand also. Reputation is very sticky. It follows you everywhere. Ask yourself what activities you are involved in, and if those who you associate with would recommend you for a hire at their company. I have seen individuals behave incredibly unprofessionally when in the bleachers at their kid's football games or at the children's school PTA meetings, for example. Just recently, I received a call from someone who was requesting a reference for a potential applicant I had previously served with on a board. This was unfortunate for the applicant because their behavior while they served on that board was unprofessional, aggressive, accusatory, and often unprepared. This person was bright and could have been the best employee, but the likelihood that their poor performance would carry into the workplace was too great to risk my *own* personal brand. You can guess what type of reference I provided. I'm certain that person never thought about their volunteer boardroom behavior becoming an obstacle in their real-life career. Although you may excuse your behavior because you are not at work, you are always being observed and your personal brand carries with you into the future. It's not enough for you to simply put your "A" game face on from 8 to 5. How you communicate differences of opinions and lobby to get your way in your volunteer and social activities stays with you for years to come. It is a segment of your brand and much more significant now with the prevalence of social media.

The same is true of your social activities. Again, act as if you are always in a job interview. Your reputation is something no one can build for you, and it follows you like gum on your shoe. So strive to have it be a positive reputation. If you make a mistake, be humble enough to own it, request forgiveness quickly, and don't let it fester. It's important that you accept grace and forgiveness when offered.

On another note, it is amazing how many people won't offer grace to those who have harmed them, and the relationship could be repaired long-term if they would. However, know that if you do your part in offering grace or forgiveness, and the receiver doesn't accept it, know it is their issue, not yours. Then move on and stay professional. There are simply some people in the world who have narcissistic behaviors and will never own their part. Don't try to force it upon this destructive type of personality.

Be cautious with controversial beliefs and topics.

So how do you build a positive brand without hurting your career when you have strong opinions around political or controversial topics? There is a place for these types of conversations and your opinions, and that is typically not the workplace. However, occasionally, conversations at the water fountain or breakroom pop up, so let me share some general advice you can follow.

I believe it is okay to take a stand and draw a line in the sand with your personal beliefs. I'm a Christian and not afraid to proclaim my faith, but I do so discreetly. As a general rule, be careful about what you share in the workplace or with those you work with. Being discreet about your opinions on controversial topics is a good guide, and remember that discretion or privacy is different from secrecy. Express that you like to be open minded with controversial topics, but refrain from the temptation of requiring everyone to agree with you. What is important is that you don't degrade other individuals because of their beliefs at any time. Be thankful of the many differences of opinions, get comfortable with saying, "I respectfully disagree and I appreciate a difference of opinion." Be cautious about taking on a rant session, especially online, as these typically have negative emotions and some type of attack contained in them that can innocently slip into the workplace. Not only that, once it's on the internet, it's there forever and you can't erase it when you change your mind later.

Most importantly, take the time to properly research what you are standing for if you want to be known as an activist, so you know the facts and you are respected by your opponents even if they don't agree with you. The media is full of false reports, manipulated stories, and fear tactics. To keep the integrity of your personal brand, you want to be sure that what you *think* you are supporting is really what you are *actually* supporting. The best thing you can do is appreciate others' views and get involved to make a difference in a positive and effective manner.

I am not generally in favor of passive aggressive approaches, such as political marches where information is insufficient, and you can't control the personal brand you create in an environment created by the group at large. Most importantly, if you complain about how our government or community leaders are making decisions, be sure you are involved at some level to help educate and serve, so you are part of the solution, not merely a finger-pointer about the problem. The same is true of your company and community events. If you have issues, ask yourself first if you had been there helping provide feedback needed for the decision, would you have actually spoken up?

As a leader, be very careful that you don't find yourself discriminating based on difference of religion, race, gender, political standpoints, or the like. This can cost you tremendous respect as a leader and hurt your personal brand. Instead, focus on skills, professionalism, and talents, rather than any factors that could be construed as discriminatory. At the same time, however, don't be held hostage to the fear of discrimination. Make the best decision based on the best candidate, as long as you believe you have made the decision fairly and in good faith, and you can hold your head high if challenged. The world is full of a victimhood mentality in this area by those whose platform isn't about proven skills and ability, and maybe more about their own minority status. If this is the case, stay keenly aware of this and focus on making the right decisions based on proven value through work ethic and who can do the best job in the position.

I always assess my decisions to be sure I am not subliminally discriminating. For example, I've always evaluated our balance of the male/female ratio and seek many demographics on my team, but I don't compromise the integrity of the process to simply hire a minority that is not qualified just because they are a minority, unless I first see the potential I would want in any hire. I have seen some people who are so passionate about a cause that they actually hurt their career and personal brand. They let their passion lead them to being so hypersensitive that they make false accusations regarding another's intentions who actually meant no harm. Educating others is a better approach, much better than making accusations. An example of this is someone who is constantly referring to a male/female factor when others receive promotions. Making comments like, "That's just because they are male," to others in the office is derogatory to the decision-making skills of the leadership and is not appropriate.

To sum it up, how you communicate on controversial subjects affects your personal brand. It's more about *how you communicate* than *what you believe*. Some of my most respected leaders and mentors have beliefs that differ strongly from mine, but I still respect them as individuals and leaders because of their integrity and strength of character. Be cautious also of when you may be baited by someone to share your view in the workplace. Sometimes silence with a smile is simply a better response.

Show up on time and be prepared.

Showing up on time to work and for meetings seems so basic, yet if not done consistently, it can cripple your personal brand as you grow your career. Poorly handling time management leaves distaste in your coworkers' and guests' mouths. Being late or unprepared leaves other people waiting on you. It wastes a good amount of the organization's money because of employees being inefficient, and it creates a poor reflection on your company. I like to refer to this as being one of those gut checks—did your behavior represent the organization and your personal brand as polished and professional? If not, go to work quickly and identify behaviors that need correction.

Also, remember that being late in your personal life can be just as damaging. Unless you move far away, the world is actually pretty connected and someone somewhere may share your reputation of always being late and it just might interfere with a job hire or promotion in the future. Cancelling meetings at the last minute is also a reflection on your brand, so do it only when it is critical to do so. Exaggerating details around why you cancelled at the last minute is also distasteful. Own it if needed and take actions to correct the situation.

Understand the impact of your lack of planning or taking on too much. It creates crisis for other people who did their own due diligence to be prepared, and it undermines your reputation. Responsible time management is a true gem in building your brand, which positively influences the building of trust and confidence in your performance at work. It can be very frustrating working with a coworker or boss who is constantly running around creating stress and anxiety because they are up against a deadline that they neglected. It instantly creates a negative brand for them because things are forced to be done quickly, which typically means it leads to mistakes or a lower-quality end result. Working under pressure almost always culminates in an oversight that can be costly to the organization, and rarely leads to the best result for all parties involved.

I have heard employees say, "I work best under pressure." If that is you, it might be true only in your own mind. Everyone else around you will strongly disagree because you "working best under pressure" provokes your team to work their last-minute worst. It can also lead to an unspoken resentment, as others are expected to drop their planned tasks or activities, with no consideration for them as they honor your projects that you believe are more important. You also create a great amount of anxiety in others who are dealing with not knowing what you have under control. If time management is a challenge on your part, take some time management classes online and get control of it quickly. There are plenty of articles online about this. Read them today and then make a commitment to change! If you are consistently running hastily into work right under the time you need to clock in, change the required time you leave your home daily. It sounds so simple, but oftentimes employees discount the importance of this on their personal brand.

Sometimes available bandwidth for the workload at hand is truly unreasonable for even the best time managers to handle. If this is affecting you, discuss it with your boss as soon as possible. Your goal is to identify together if you have an unreasonable workload or if there is something you can improve. The reason you should discuss it as soon as possible is to allow time for solutions or help. Approach the discussion with an accounting of your time and the tasks you are working on each day, so you have some factual information to share as a part of that discussion. Then discuss a solution.

I've always said that if you feel overwhelmed with an unreasonable workload, it is your responsibility to bring it to your supervisor's attention so you can work together on a solution. They can help you prioritize and assess the situation. Sometimes your boss doesn't pay close attention to your daily activities, so they may not even be aware, especially if your normal demeanor is agreeable and cooperative. You owe it to them to have the discussion. It could be a situation that you work more slowly than others or aren't working efficiently. Don't take this defensively if it is the case. Instead, own it, and discuss goals to overcome it. This builds mutual respect as well as improves the immediate situation. If you have time management issues in the workplace, it often carries over as a challenge in providing sufficient lead time with announcements and communications within the company as well, so it is important for you and your boss to be aware of what is really happening, and then get started on solutions.

One final thing on time management that I see creep into the workplace is the decision to work overtime, adding an expense to your company. I encourage you to seek your supervisor's help in avoiding overtime, unless they have requested it. I've seen employees stretch their workload to pick up a few hours of overtime in a week. It's a very bad practice that hurts your brand. Find every way possible to avoid overtime and work as a team to become efficient in this area. It oftentimes is a poor time management practice or an intentional decision in order to add pay to your paycheck. If you can become proactive about avoiding overtime where possible, you will send a strong signal to your supervisor that you care about protecting the company's resources and will always act in the best interest of your company: two huge traits that will provide value in building your brand. Get aggressive at avoiding overtime and leading your teams to do the same. Show your team that you are willing to put in extra effort if needed, but don't demand overtime to be able to step it up a little if you can accomplish more within your normal work hours. Getting good at this will serve you well, because as you get promoted, you will certainly become salaried at some point. Being on salary has many benefits, but being paid for overtime is generally not one of them.

Work ethic shows up in many places.

First and foremost, employees who want to move ahead should never forget who they work for and who dishes out the resources for their paycheck. Employers expect employees to support them with their actions, words, reputations, and commitment while at work. In one period early in my career, I worked alongside a peer with tremendous talent and watched her get passed over for promotions as she ignorantly justified her poor work ethic around personal phone calls and arriving late often. She had sadly hit a brick wall by her own doing. Stay off your cell phones unless you need to be watching them for work purposes. Don't browse social media or the sports updates during work. Use your break times for what they are intended to be used for, a time for a good mental break from work and to address personal needs. Simply put, bosses don't want to promote slackers who will lead others to be slackers. Avoid that 15-minute personal chitchat with a coworker when on the clock. You just cost the company 30-minutes (15 minutes of your time and 15 minutes of the other's time) of work that didn't get done. Others notice this! And don't whine when your employer reinforces rules around work ethic and efficient use of employees' time. Employers dislike whiners because they don't make trusted leaders who can resolve difficult situations.

Sometimes, it's not easy to make personal sacrifices in the face of work ethic when your company simply needs you to fill a need or role. But there are times you simply have to put your employer first. They likely put you first often, such as paying payroll over other expenses when funds are tight, for example. You improve your personal brand when you show you are willing to make a sacrifice, and balance it with also taking care of yourself and your family.

I recall a merger day one New Year's holiday many years ago when my husband and a group of friends were headed to their first bowl game with the Boise State Broncos, my favorite college football team. Unfortunately, I was not able to join in the fun because of the merger weekend, of which I was responsible for leading part of the conversion. Fortunately, I had a more important job to do at work that weekend instead. I didn't like it, but understood and supported it, and I knew it was not the norm. It was an investment in my career, both present and future, and it paid off in the long run.

Speak truth into unethical or compromising situations.

It's just as important to your brand what you speak truth into when things are happening that you know are ethically wrong. "See something, say something," is good advice when you see something you know the leadership would want to know that is just not right. So what if you have a strong intuition but no facts at this time that something may be unethical and contrary to your organization's value statements? Sometimes gut is the most powerful intuitive observation to get any investigation about a serious concern started. However, it's important to present the situation as a gut feeling if that's all it actually is. It's also important to stay unemotional as best as you can, and find ways where it doesn't become personal. It's critical that you are willing to be in a follow-up conversation to clarify, even if that conversation might be an uncomfortable one.

Earlier in my career, I made the tough decision to take an issue up the ladder, knowing my job may be on the line or I may become uncomfortable if the board handled it poorly or my boss reacted unfairly. Even so, I was invested in doing the right thing, even if the immediate outcome wasn't what I wanted, to protect my reputation and brand, and to be able to sleep at night with a good conscience. I was also resolved that when I spoke up, if management handled it poorly, it would not likely be a company I would want to continue to invest my career in. I made peace with my replaceability. I had an obligation as an employee of that company to bring it to the attention of upper management. Fortunately, it went better than I anticipated and I will never regret taking that risk, because it was based on facts and clearly identified actions that did not support the company's mission. I planned the conversation carefully so it included unbiased facts and was presented in an unemotional and professional way. I also encouraged the leadership to complete their own investigation and not take my personal view as the only perspective. I then stepped aside and let them take the action they felt appropriate in their investigation, and committed to trust the process, fully aware that if that process wronged me, I could (and would) part ways.

Happily, when all was said and done, I could not have asked for a better outcome. Years later, I was told that the approach I took in how I handled that situation was impressive and they gained confidence in my abilities as a leader, which eventually paid off with my next big promotion. Was it hard and uncomfortable? Absolutely! Did it take tremendous courage? A resounding yes! I lost many hours of sleep and had more butterflies than I could count swarming in my stomach. The anxiety was high. It was painfully hard. But, was it the right thing to do? Also a resounding yes! My personal brand and reputation actually improved with this experience, and had I chosen not to speak up, I ran the risk of being accused of being a participant of the wrongdoing, since I held the role of the VP Finance and was ultimately responsible.

Leave on good terms when you leave an employer, regardless of the situation.

Simply stated, don't trash or break confidentiality with your employer, boss, or coworker on the way out the door. When you leave a company, it is important you support them in whatever manner you can, even if you left because of an involuntary termination or a disappointing situation. How you handle the communication regarding why you left a previous employer is critical to maintaining a professional brand and your actions could follow you through to the next career choice in a big way.

Never burn your bridges on the way out. Never! Stay positive and support the things your company did for you, such as what you learned, even from bad situations. I remember being in an exit interview years ago, and when asked why I was leaving, I simply stated something similar to, "I have no intention of being negative on my way out the door. You have provided me many great benefits and I am choosing to stay positive and grateful for what you provided. There is nothing I have to say that hasn't already been said, and I prefer to stay positive and leave on great terms. I would never want to harm this company. It is my hope I can always be appreciative for what you have provided to me." You will kill your brand if you slam your previous employer, and especially if you go out of your way to steal their employees or give away confidential trade secrets that you know were meant to be confidential, such as sharing a customer list or schematics to a program.

In general, be less selfish about what you want to gain in the form of retaliation or what you want to "prove" to any company you leave. And please, this is not the time to be passive aggressive. Never fire off a nastygram after you leave to the owner, corporate office, or the board of directors. It's more important that you gave them the chance to sit down with you and discuss your issues with them prior to your leaving the company. And then let them own whatever actions they then choose to take.

There are always exceptions to this rule, and I would say that would be when there is unethical, illegal, or immoral activity, and stepping up to do what is right is the courageous thing to do. But if it doesn't fall into one of these three categories, deal with it through solid face-to-face communication, and then let it be and change your own course if the company chooses to ignore the situation. There may be a very good reason (that you may never find out) that they are ignoring your recommendation, such as it doesn't fit the direction the owner wants to go, but letting them own it instead of you is my best advice.

I could give you many case studies where an employee leaves because it wasn't a good fit and they are dissatisfied, and then they turn to the passive aggressive approach and proactively try to influence the existing employees, or send a nastygram that is exaggerated and unfair. I have seen employees cause a serious reputation risk and concern about their intentions and professionalism by backstabbing their previous employer, especially if their motivation is to take them down. I have seen some rare and ugly situations that hurt an employee because of these kinds of poor choices. In one case, the community even stepped forward to defend my company, shared the bad rumors with me, and then stated that this person was already known as someone who "leaves companies and tries to leave a pile of bodies in her wake." Do you want to be known as a person who does that? I hope not. In the end, the only one that typically gets hurt in this situation is the backstabber, and it can create long-term pain for a short-term selfish gain.

So you might ask yourself, why would someone take this negative and destructive approach on their way out the door? If they are leaving anyway, why do they care? I believe it is to bolster their own self-validation as to why they are no longer working for that employer. People's identity is often in whom they work for. Right or wrong, if an ex-employee can create a believable story that will justify their decision to leave that employer, it immediately makes them feel justified when people ask why they left or changed jobs.

In summary, they behave this way to avoid owning that they made a poor career choice, were under-performing, or in over their head. They take on the victim role and want to create other victims who agree with them. Another reason ex-employees behave poorly with negativity after they leave is to sell their case and keep connections with those on the inside, because their curiosity is greater than their desire to move on and build their career going forward. It makes them feel better if they can rally a tribe to support their decision to leave. Or, they may simply want to have power over their previous peers, employees, or the company.

In the end, you simply need to protect your ability to receive an honest and good reference from your previous employer. There are dozens of ways to get the inside scoop on an employee through acquaintances, social media, etc., even if you don't list them as references. Therefore, always leave owning what you should and communicating in a manner that will allow your previous boss to share your strengths and character values, regardless of your performance.

Some often ask what they should say about a previous difficult boss or company when they are interviewing. I recommend you be honest and gentle with what you share, but be very clear what the positive attributes were and what you learned. You need to be honest with how you handled it, how you could have handled it better, and what you gained from the experience. Don't belabor the negative, but speak to it if you believe there is a chance it will be discovered through reference checks or casual acquaintance inquiries. If the story holds true, it is often an acceptable item for recruiters to accept and should lead to additional clarifying questions. But, don't be dramatic or slanderous. Recruiters are often trained to pick up on body language when stories don't jive, so don't lie. Even if they don't discover something important in an interview, it is just as dangerous when it is discovered months later when you are an employee. You don't want to set yourself up for distrust.

So when you change employers, always respect the employer you left: They gave you a chance and invested in you at some level, and burning that bridge will most likely sabotage your career.

Carry a physical presence that looks like you own the part.

Remember that first impression is critical with how you are judged. How you dress, maintain eye contact, and sit in a meeting has an impact with the brand people give you. If you slump on your elbow or recline back in your office chair in an important meeting, it creates a less-than-desired brand for you. Those around you will ask if you really want to be there. The same is true if you are constantly looking at your cell phone or the floor. Make strong eye contact when you are talking to someone and be sure you perfect a good handshake. If you carry a whimsical or lackadaisical demeanor throughout the office, one would assume you will do the same if they put you in charge of a new department or project. If you yawn and appear disengaged when your boss or someone else is giving a presentation, even if it is the most boring presentation you've ever sat through and you were up late last night, fake it and carry yourself as if you are genuinely interested. What works for me when I'm in that useless presentation is to take notes, even if I toss them when I leave the room. And certainly pay attention to dressing for the job you desire, not adopting the minimum dress code standards in place today. Always dress up one position in the company, even if you take some teasing by your peers.

3: Use Difficult Moments as Learning Opportunities

Stick through tough situations. Every job has a bad day, bad boss, and bad customer on occasion.

No job is perfect. Let me say this again because it is important:

NO JOB IS PERFECT.

No company is perfect. No boss is perfect. No office is perfect. No team is perfect. I have seen so many employees leave a job because of a dislike with something in the organization that had recently changed or that they didn't care for. It could be a new supervisor, coworker, or work space. Maybe the specifics around their new job aren't exactly what they imagined. They are unable to see the potential within the company and their future strategic growth opportunity, and therefore they make a short-term decision to flee, oftentimes regretting it later. I've had employees call me within weeks after leaving my organizations over the years, expressing their regret in their decision to leave, how they left, or why they made their decision to leave. The grass is not always greener on the other side. Every company has its own imperfections. Identify them, find ways to improve them, and own your own part to make it better. Stop complaining and, instead, commit to finding ways to make each situation work for you and the company. Whiners lose respect quickly.

Quick Sabotage Assessment: Am I willing to learn from and stick through the tough days? Every job has them.

CAREER BUILDING CHARACTERISTICS	Y/N	CAREER SABOTAGING CHARACTERISTICS	Y/N
Do I take an undesirable situation that happened today and turn it into an opportunity to problem solve?		Do I become easily frustrated when things don't go my way and go to an "I'm outta here" mode? Do I often ask to change departments or leave my current employer when things aren't to my liking?	
Do I find a way to show leadership and communication skills to fix a problem when one occurs?		Do I get frustrated and lean on my boss to fix things and expect them to notice everything that goes wrong?	
Am I proactively looking for areas where I can use my skills and help the company improve, well before something goes wrong?		Am I reactive when something goes wrong and even worse, add my negative attitude to the situation?	
Do I look for ways to "coach up" and help my boss become more successful?		Do I expect my boss to be perfect and share with others when he/she makes a mistake?	
Do I find the courage to say what needs to be said in a supportive and solution-based manner and seek to understand whenever possible?		Do I gossip about people and situations because I am not willing to step into the conversation I need to be a part of? Do I try to get others to complain for me?	
Do I address my dissatisfaction with my job or career in a professional and non-threatening manner?		Do I build my list of bullets on my way out the door to fire away in my exit interview, and do the bullets include things I have not given my boss an opportunity to correct or understand? Do I give my boss ultimatums regarding my career?	

(Quick Sabotage Assessment, Cont.)

CAREER BUILDING CHARACTERISTICS	Y/N	CAREER SABOTAGING CHARACTERISTICS	Y/N
Do I take advantage of my personal coaching sessions and performance review meetings to speak the truth in a professional manner?		*Do I say everything is fine when it is actually not fine, simply because I hate conflict?*	
Do I give the leadership of my company the benefit of doubt and find a way to support their direction with new rollouts and changes?		*Am I immediately skeptical and require others to get me on board with the new direction of the company?*	
Do I stay positive when stuff hits the fan?		*Am I a whiner and complainer when things don't go as planned?*	
Do I report unethical, immoral, or illegal activity as soon as I discover it and do so with facts? Do I allow the management some space to properly investigate, and then trust their decision from that process when I do?		*Do I spread the word about my findings to other employees who have no reason to know? Am I unwilling to share my observations with those responsible to know because of a fear of retaliation, and then let the bad behavior of others continue? And then do I keep gossiping about it?*	

Let me share one of my personal experiences that singlehandedly was one of the best decisions I made in my career. I own this and celebrate it because it was not easy. In fact, it was almost unbearable at times.

Years ago, I took a different VP Finance position for a company after I left a career of 12 years at the Girl Scouts. It was a company that doesn't exist anymore, so let's call it Company X for the purpose of this story. What is relevant about Company X was its dysfunction and challenges. Immediately—literally on my first day—I observed an environment where employees distrusted management, had no direction, were micromanaged, and the employee roster consisted of almost every family relationship imaginable. There were parents and their children, in-laws, and significant others working together, which led to an environment that contained family cat fights and extreme inconsistency with accountability and expectations in performance. Nepotism can be ugly and destructive, and it was certainly that way there. Then there were the rest of us, who were not related, and most of us were not part of the dysfunction.

My first week was a tremendous letdown, because I expected this to be the start of my new dream career and learning a new industry I believed I could build a great career around. And remember, I had just left a great career in a nurturing environment for a wonderful cause-driven non-profit organization after 12 years. Unfortunately, at Company X, there were daily thought-provoking moments that required being broken down and unraveled to their simplest forms in order to even begin to address them. I had a team of accounting staff who wanted to perform well, and my immediate job was to shelter them from the dysfunction as best I could, while also being supportive of management among them. The messaging of our situations stayed focused on how best to work in this environment professionally and stay positive with the impact we could have in our own circle of influence to improve the company. But then it got worse.

Without going into the many gory details, let's just say it was an environment that would be justified in escaping. I could have accepted this justification and ran from Company X and their bad environment and returned to my prior safe job, as they begged to have me return. But I knew there were things I could learn at Company X that I could never learn at the Girl Scouts. So, I took a different approach and stayed for the opportunity. I set a personal goal that I would coach up (meaning I would help lead my boss, knowing I was in a lower position in the organization chart). I also set a goal that I would coach sideways with my peers, and another goal to coach and love on my employees who had been through a great deal of dysfunction and a horrible culture. I immediately went to work on what I could control and positively influence, identified which relationships were safe to approach, and slowly we improved the working environment piece by piece. Lengthy conversations occurred in my mind as I would imagine how best to word them, and how to have tough conversations without putting people on the defense. I would process how to ensure I was fulfilling my role as a top executive, responsible for the financial affairs and setting the example of effective leadership in this organization. This was no easy task.

What I didn't know during all this was that the most difficult time was still to come. After gradually improving one policy and practice after another, it slowly became apparent that some unethical practices existed, on top of all the poor culture and dysfunction. This is when it became real! Again, I had perfect justification to resign from Company X. I sought out advice from a trusted Human Resource professional, and then made the decision that I needed to take the information I discovered and report it to the board of directors. If not me, then who would? I wondered if anyone had observed such practices in the past but chose to stay silent. It took me a month to get the courage to step forward, regardless of the outcome, because it was the right thing to do for the employer that was paying me to perform as an executive. And I did it. Soon after, an investigation was completed and a change in leadership occurred at Company X. The repairs began.

I share this because even in the worst of situations, my staying with the company was the right thing to do for me and my career. I learned skills I could not learn anywhere else, and I use these skills to this day.

It is important to also talk about what would have happened if the unethical behavior continued and my communication of the situation fell on deaf ears. This is important to assess when you are in this situation, as you have no guarantee how it might be handled by the leadership of your organization. For me, I know I would have eventually left the company if it became apparent there was no chance of them showing they held a value system compatible with mine. But it's important not to jump away until you see the outcome. I chose to stay through the process, in order for the leadership and board of directors to have sufficient time to properly address the situation. My goal was not to get the CEO fired: My goal was to improve the organization and get the unethical behavior to stop, regardless of who was CEO.

Organizations have inertia. You can't turn a cruise ship on a dime. Every decision has ripple effects. It's important not to demand or expect a radical change overnight when you file a complaint, but give the leadership enough time to understand the situation and work through the necessary coaching and investigative process. Sometimes employees get so caught up in controlling the situation and pushing management to get the apparent violator fired that they lose perspective of their own responsibility and behave poorly. You can't own your supervisor's decisions all the time. Give everyone some space after you communicate some difficult observations to any leadership person in charge in order for them to self-assess, properly observe the complaint themselves, verify the facts, and then decide on the best appropriate action. Know that it takes time to properly research and assess any situation, especially a complaint about integrity or general leadership behavior, so provide the space. This will prevent you from making a rash decision and leaving the company because you "don't think they are doing anything to improve the situation."

Much happens at the upper management level that employees never hear anything about, and I say this to you because you may someday appreciate the same methodical process if you are ever falsely accused by someone who complains to your leadership about you. I have been on the accused side and was grateful the company took their time, methodically investigated, and found that the complaint was not valid. In that situation, I respect how the board handled that unfortunate situation, which was to carefully consider the entire complaint to ensure they were not acting solely on one-sided input or one person's emotions.

There are always two sides to every situation and complaint. After all, I could have been wrong or misinterpreted the situation at Company X. Anyone could be, so to expect management to instantly believe your issues and take immediate action is simply not fair to either party. If you handle this carefully and with facts only, it's the best you can do. Then trust the process and let it work. The worst course of action to take is to jump ship without letting the process work for a positive outcome. Why? Because, now you start all over again in your career and have to build trust with a new team. And don't ever be passive aggressive about your complaints in the process or you will instantly lose credibility, a loss that will follow you forever.

Company X eventually merged into a new company and then dissolved. After that, I was fortunate to be hired by Icon Credit Union, formerly Idahy FCU, where I recently celebrated 20 years of an amazing career. I worked my way from a VP of Finance to today's CEO.

The reason I share this story is that I could have left several times in that prior poor culture of a company and gone back to my safe zone at the Girl Scouts, a job that I loved, but also one where I had exhausted the opportunities to expand my career. By owning my own career, sticking through the tough times, and learning through them, I gained tremendous skills in what difficult conversations look like, how to stay impartial and unemotional when emotions run high, and even better, what type of environment I never wanted to work in again.

I have become passionate about building a strong culture and using it to my competitive advantage. I know if I had jumped ship, I would never have had the opportunity to come to Icon Credit Union as their VP of Finance, because I had worked closely through the dysfunction at Company X with Icon's board treasurer. Unbeknownst to me, in our small world, he was observing and watching how I carried myself and the decisions I made in that dysfunctional environment. At the time, he was also the CEO of where I am employed today. Years later, he shared that even though there were other candidates for the VP of Finance position that were more technically qualified for the position, he had seen me work professionally through difficult situations and I made an impact on his view of my communication and professional skills. If I would have left during the dysfunction, I would have never had the wonderful opportunity I get to lead the great organization I am in today, and it is an incredible one.

Know that when you start over with a new employer, you have a higher risk of truly having to start over in your career. You must learn new policies, new relationships, new expectations, and will face new obstacles. Each time you change companies, especially for a lateral move, you run a risk of setting back your career. Each step in my career advanced me to the next level, but they didn't always mean an employer change. In fact, most did not. Ask yourself before you make a move if you are simply running from what is a temporary and difficult situation you can grow from, or a permanent one that will never change. Bad bosses do come and go, some just take a little longer for management to scope out than others. The bad ones that stay too long almost always stay because the team is not courageous enough to work through crucial conversations.

So what dislikes do you have that you can work through with some determination that will make you stronger and a better leader in your current job? After all, moving up the ladder in any organization brings on new challenges and environments where you will need these skills, and everything becomes a little more complex. It all takes strong communication skills to succeed, and perfecting these is a wise investment. How can you gain new communication skills while working through difficult situations and stay where you are, getting ready to advance to the next position? My recommendation is to look at your challenges through a new lens, and ask how you can shine through these challenges while staying with the same company (if possible). You will have an impressive impact on the confidence your boss has in you. And even better, you will gain tremendous respect when you are the one who steps up and professionally addresses situations that need help. Showing courage with good intention builds respect, and it becomes easier each time you do it. Shift your thinking and ask yourself, "How can I make a positive impact today and build my courageous leadership skills in the process?"

Some employees leave strictly for money. My advice is to be careful when this happens, and look at the opportunity you are walking away from in the future. Let's say you can make $1.00 more an hour if you move from Company A to Company B. That's usually $2,080/year if you work 40 hours/week. Now take out taxes and estimate the impact of your take-home pay and how much it really adds to your household budget. Now look at the benefits offered by the two companies and put an annual hourly rate to them for the important ones, such as medical insurance. Don't lose sight of what incentives or bonus plan you may be able to capitalize on to increase your compensation if you stay there. And the most important factor is what the opportunity is for you to increase pay with the next logical promotion in the two companies, and how much of a raise will come with that promotion.

Employees are simply jumping around too much today and you are likely to have a spot open up with your present employer before you even expect it if you are a valuable employee, increasing your pay with the next advancement. Estimate the number of months it will likely take for you to get a promotion at both companies, and then break that down to an hourly rate to properly evaluate.

This is important as well...know that you only have to make as much as you spend. So ask yourself if you can cut your spending in order to have the same "net" effect and stay with the same company until the next opportunity comes to fruition. Have an open dialogue with your supervisor to assess the opportunities. Then make the best decision, considering all the facts beyond the basic $1.00/hour. I have had many opportunities to sit with an employee and complete this analysis, and clearly show that they are better off sitting tight until a promotion is in order. In much fewer situations, the opportunity has shown worthy of a move, but going through this exercise will enlighten the knowledge around this decision. What I don't recommend is using a competitor's offer as an ultimatum to increase your pay at your current job. It can work sometimes without resentment, but it is typically a short-term solution and often creates future problems. Your lack of loyalty to the company and the questionable reason you work there (e.g. only for the money) can cause some distrust and future concern about promoting you to higher positions, because your commitment may be in question.

Let me share a personal example of exploring another career opportunity and how receiving a lower financial salary in my current position worked in my favor fifteen years ago. I was recruited to apply for a CEO position in another local credit union that was smaller than where I currently worked. I was currently a VP of Finance, making much less than that potential CEO position was offering. I interviewed for the position, but before I ever went to the interview, I notified my current CEO that I was going to apply because I was recruited and was grateful for the opportunity to check it out. It was important for me not to shut my ears to potential rewarding opportunities like this, even though I wasn't looking, and I encourage you to do the same. Now, it's important to note that I had built a trusted relationship with my CEO and I knew I could have this conversation about applying and have it go well (and you will, too, if you follow the guidance in this book). If I had not nurtured my work ethic, career, personal brand, and professional relationships, I would not have been invited to such an opportunity, nor would I have been able to have such a profitable conversation with my boss. I had full confidence that my performance was stellar and he would not want me to resign. He did what any good boss would do and encouraged me to check it out, but also asked that I please talk to him before I made a decision. After I was offered the position, I met with him to share the exciting opportunity, as it was one I seriously wanted to pursue. I never asked for more money in that meeting, but he offered me a nice raise to stay anyway.

Now, some take this as being offended that if he was willing to pay me that, why was he not already doing so? I don't look at it that way. Business is business. I accepted my current job for a certain salary several years ago and I received regular raises. So it isn't my employer's fault that another company came in out of the blue and offered me much more for a more complex and different role. He and I worked the numbers together as to what I could eventually be making in five years as our company grew, the value of our culture, and other important factors. I knew the work environment I held at that time was a good one. I also knew the work environment I might be stepping into was an unknown, including their team and board of directors and how they worked. The numbers worked out where it was worth the risk to stay put and push that differential between the two situations into the future, far exceeding what my potential was in the new CEO offer. And it has proven to be one of the best decisions I have made in my career. I didn't chase the title and money: I chased potential and then worked hard to fulfil it with my current employer. In looking back, I'm also not sure I was quite ready for a CEO position at that time. Investing the next five years to be truly ready in a much larger institution was a smart investment for me.

According to *thebalancecareers.com*, the average person changes jobs **ten to fifteen times** (with an average of 12 job changes) during his or her career. Many workers spend five years or less in every job, so they devote even more time and energy transitioning from one job to another. In January 2016, the Bureau of Labor Statistics reported the average employee tenure was 4.2 years, down from 4.6 years in January 2014. Take advantage of this staggering statistic that is sabotaging careers and continues to get worse. There is a tremendous advantage to being one of the employees who patiently works through career planning and challenges. You will shine at the end of your journey, and will gain communication and strategic skills that many others won't possess.

Don't make the crucial mistake of chasing a perfect employer or boss. If it were that easy, everyone would be landing in the same company. Instead, fight like heck to make your current employer work for you if you see a shared value system and potential. And, of course, never leave without giving your employer a chance to improve if you are leaving for something that is fixable or has the potential of improving. You will learn from every situation, and that knowledge is powerful and can't be learned by reading a book. Again, know there are exceptions to every situation, so take this advice as relevant in most normal companies who are often growing leaders and dealing with ongoing complex problems.

4: Shut Down the Drama Zone

Creating or participating in drama and gossip are surefire ways to block your career. This is *your career*, not a reality TV show. Drama can take on many forms, and you'll likely know it when you see it because it takes on undesirable behaviors that lead to creating self-centered, immature, and uncomfortable spectacles and commotions. Stop being a drama king or queen. It's a horrible coping mechanism that will sabotage your career. It's also unattractive and sucks the life out of those around you. I am not only going to address how you personally can prevent getting sucked into drama, which will gain you great respect, but also how you can impact your entire organization to create a "no drama zone."

Employees who are able to master this skill are typically great communicators and dependable employees because they know how to fully own their performance and not get sidetracked by trivialities. Trust from team members builds quickly for them. In addition, they typically are more satisfied in life because they don't get bogged down with others' problems or victimhood scapegoating. Not only do they know how to own their responsibilities in the workplace, they are simply better at building healthy relationships with employees who want to work in an environment with a great culture.

Plain and simple, drama = poor culture. No one wants to work in a toxic work environment, so avoid being a player in one.

Quick Sabotage Assessment: Do I avoid drama by communicating in a manner that doesn't create it?

CAREER BUILDING CHARACTERISTICS	Y/N	CAREER SABOTAGING CHARACTERISTICS	Y/N
Do I create a presence in the office that I will not partake in any conversation intended to simply talk poorly about a coworker?		*As soon as something undesirable happens in the office, or someone makes a mistake, do I share this with others in the office who have no real reason to be informed?*	
Do I ask good, solution-focused questions of those who bring me their problems?		*Do I just want to vent about personal characteristics, rather than get advice on real solutions I am willing to courageously take on?*	
When I am upset, do I communicate fairly with those who have the power to change the situation?		*Do I share my frustration with those who are not responsible to fix the problem?*	
Do I set healthy boundaries, while still being empathetic, to avoid enabling a victim bringing drama into the workplace?		*Am I codependent and help more than I should with a victim-type personality? Do I become resentful for how much I am being asked to help and not stand up for myself to set healthy boundaries? Do I make my rescuers, and those trying to help, feel guilty when they set boundaries?*	
Do I stay supportive of management when others complain to me?		*Do I join in and share my own frustrations when others in the office complain about someone or something?*	

(Quick Sabotage Assessment, Cont.)

CAREER BUILDING CHARACTERISTICS	Y/N	CAREER SABOTAGING CHARACTERISTICS	Y/N
When I bring something to my supervisor's attention that others are feeling, do I bring them with me in the conversation or schedule a meeting so they can share firsthand their concerns?		*Do I let myself become the messenger of others to deliver concerns, and refuse to tell them they need to address their concerns without me?*	
Do I keep my personal problems out of my work life and responsibilities?		*Do I bring my personal relationship or other problems to work and talk bad about my spouse or others to my coworkers, causing a distraction and inefficient use of time?*	
Do I squash all rumors going around and request the messenger to stop the gossip? Do I keep what I hear to myself when petty complaining or personal attacks occur?		*Do I spread the rumors when I hear them with my coworker friends?*	
Am I careful to share the full details when discussing a potential issue or concern?		*Do I leave out important pieces of the situation to unfairly influence the listener?*	

In order to first talk about drama, it is important to fully understand what causes it. I had the privilege of learning from Abe Wagner several years ago about the roles that people play that create drama. He provided the great visual below to illustrate the Drama Triangle. Let's break down each of these three roles in detail and discuss how drama is created when any two of these three roles choose to engage with each other.

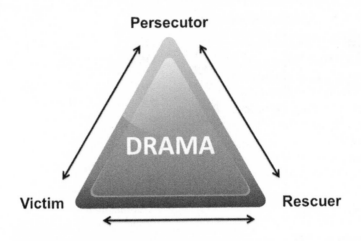

1. **Persecutor**
2. **Victim**
3. **Rescuer**

So let's discuss each of the three roles. If two people choose to interact within these roles, drama is created, as well as many other horrible situations, such as codependency, retaliation, passive-aggressive approaches, and resentment.

The Persecutor

The first role is known as the **persecutor**, which is a person who tends to control through intimidation. They show unnecessary anger on occasion, make unreasonable demands, and they often prey on victims because they can control them through their persecution techniques. Persecutors can be resistant to giving their employees the time and attention they need, while then criticizing them when the work is not done right. Persecutors tend to have poor listening skills because they are framing their response quickly and typically without a thought of the impact on their audience from their message. They can be vocal sticklers with the rules even when reality indicates it would be logical to make an exception.

Persecutors create drama because they tend to hit a nerve of their prey and criticize personally. What is interesting and important to note is that most drama that is initiated by persecutors does not extend over long periods of time. Employees are willing to stand up for themselves more often when they interact with a persecutor than the other two roles on this triangle. It's also easy for employees to justify leaving an organization if the persecutor is not addressed by management, especially if the persecutor *is* the management. Persecutor-type behaviors are often noticeably unacceptable in the workplace and employees are often protected with language included in the personnel policies. More often than not, the employee who interacts with a persecutor feels safe taking the inappropriate situation to their supervisor or the Human Resources Department. However, the same is not true of the other two roles, the rescuer and victim.

The Victim

The second role in the drama triangle is the **victim**. Employees who play the victim card create a significant amount of drama in the workplace, often unknowingly. They may be hardworking and talented employees with extreme skills, but often lack the ability to bypass obstacles that come their way or own their individual challenges or problems. Victims are whiny and can be pathetic with their woes. They can be ill-equipped to work through any type of conflict and often refuse to stand up for themselves. They are very drawn to rescuers (described below), who carry the role of a listener who wants to help without pushing the victim to own their problems. The victim loves to get attention from caring and empathetic listeners and providers. Victims have a difficult time asking themselves, "What is my part?" or "What is my responsibility to correct this situation?"

Victims love to present themselves as helpless and may blame the company for not recognizing or fixing their needs or challenges. The blame game is their best friend: Many victims have mastered this game. They can name every person who has ever harmed them, but they rarely share and own about all the people they themselves have harmed. If they had a dysfunctional childhood or an alcoholic parent, for example, you'll know it, because they will share it, most often when they have a challenge they need to own themselves. They'll use their misfortunes as the justification for their behavior when they aren't performing at their fullest or expected potential. They may blame their refusal to build relationships in the workplace on having an alcoholic parent, for example. Or they may blame their inability to be flexible and do the job at work on being a single mother. I could give dozens of victim examples. These are only a few.

55

Not all people who have had unfortunate situations should be labelled as victims in the workplace. Instead, many use their unfortunate situation or experiences to make a difference in their world and find determination to overcome their challenges to create a great work environment. Being a victim in this drama-creating role is more about if the employee plays the card as an excuse or blames the boss or management's decisions as a reason to be disgruntled, negative, or refuse to support the direction. Having a victim mentality at work is a choice. Victims don't like solutions or others' disagreements with them when they feel wronged. Quite frankly, they want you to feel sorry for them. Helpful souls eventually risk becoming their victim, too, especially when they set boundaries or participate in their whiny gossip. A sense of ownership is typically low with victim mentalities, and as a result, they can suck the life out of those who will listen. It is exhausting to supervisors who have victims on their teams.

Victims prey on rescuers. If the supervisor is also a rescuer mentality, this can be a dangerous relationship and will most likely cause both of their careers to be sabotaged. Victims know who in the organization is willing to listen with compassion and empathy. Even more so, victims find rescuers who love harmony, because that lends itself to lengthy conversations about how people feel and how the rescuer can make the victim feel better. Victims enjoy watching a rescuer feel important while the rescuer is providing advice. It makes them feel like they now have a confidant, a partner, to share in their woes and feel sorry for them. Victims also build a tribe and receive great satisfaction when they can team up with two rescuers. Double the prize!

Victims also become dependent on the rescuer. They depend on the rescuer to process their feelings and provide advice. Unfortunately, the victim hates solutions, so this creates a long-term unhealthy relationship. What's interesting is the rescuer typically doesn't know how and when to exit the relationship to help the victim solve their own problems, especially if they are a peer.

Here are some common phrases victims will use. Listen for these in the workplace and assess the employee's capability to own their performance when you hear them.

- "Why does everything keep happening to me?"
- "When it rains, it pours."

- "That wouldn't work. I've already tried that."
- "It wouldn't do any good."
- "They won't listen to me, even if I did talk to them."
- "Why doesn't my supervisor notice the problem?"
- "They just don't care."

You see, victims hate solutions. When you give them advice that requires an action on their part, and they want to stay in victimhood, taking that action might actually pull them out of being a victim. Therefore, they will sabotage the recommended action so they can continue to play the victim card. It's sad, but it happens more than we realize in the workplace. What is also unfortunate is that victims will sometimes turn to persecution techniques against the rescuer if that employee refuses to help them or not offer to co-own their problems, oftentimes when the victim is completely capable of handling the situation themselves.

The Rescuer

Now, let's introduce you to the third role in the drama triangle, the **rescuer.** Bless their hearts. These are the kind, well meaning, caring, wise, sensitive individuals in your organization. They are the employees who love harmony and can't stand to see anything out of sorts. Rescuers are fixers, but they often don't fix the right problem. The rescuers love to help and provide compassionate advice where they feel someone will listen, especially where it helps an underserved or underprivileged individual.

It's also good to understand that rescuers have a difficult time setting boundaries because they want to feel important, and their identity often lies within whom they are helping. Rescuers are often codependents and also good listeners. The description of a codependent is *"the unhealthy physiological reliance of one person on another."* The unhealthy part of this is that it can go on for years and create obstacles in the workplace in communication, accountability, and identifying solutions.

So what is an example of an unhealthy reliance? It could be when an employee is willing to have their door open to the employee who needs to emotionally process their issues repeatedly in order to find fulfillment at work. In this situation, it's unhealthy because the conversation typically contains more gossip than the victim's willingness to take action to improve and own their situation. If the victim didn't have the rescuer to communicate with, they would keep looking to find another rescuer.

Another term for rescuer is "enabler." Enablers are the supporters and helpers in the organization. Unfortunately, rescuers also hurt the organization, often unintentionally and innocently. They feel like they have the gift of compassion and it's their responsibility to use that gift and be there for the hurting employees who are struggling. Unfortunately, if they aren't equipped to handle the conversation or situation correctly, they end up becoming victims themselves. They can now be flagged as one of the office gossip crew. You see, the victim will use every opportunity to explain the "sound advice" they received from the rescuer, because after all, the victim is building their rescuer tribe to fight their battles, even if ever so small. Once the rescuer refuses to bring a victim's situation to the attention of their supervisor when it is detrimental to the company, the rescuer then becomes known as someone who does not act in the best interest of the company. The supervisor may ask, "If you knew that was a problem or they were complaining about that, why didn't you bring it to my attention?" That's a fair question.

So what do you think happens to the rescuer the next time a promotion is on the table? They will likely get passed over because the leadership team cannot trust that they will care more about the greater good of the company than themselves or supporting the victim. This is where the rescuers good intentions fall to victimhood, right along with the victim. The leadership will see the rescuer protect the victim and even hide other employees' inadequacies, when it's better that management know where there are gaps in employee performance. Rescuers often put their own personal emotions and feelings over company needs. They want to be the hero for their employees, but instead they create the hero stigma by holding back their employees from growth.

Let me be clear that the victim, for the purposes of this chapter, is not the employee who had something unfortunate happen to them where they became an actual victim as a result of an action completely out of their control. For example, this may include being sexually harassed at work when they have been diligent in clearly stating the personnel policies and their boundaries. True victims have a responsibility to immediately bring the unfortunate situation, which was out of their control, to their supervisor. The victims discussed in this chapter are those who have some control to fix their situation, but aren't willing to take the action needed to do so. This might include an employee not completing their work or missing deadlines, but not willing to seek help with priorities to address the situation. Another example might be an employee who doesn't understand a new process, but only complains and doesn't seek additional training. Sometimes, it's simply complaining about the personality differences with their team or boss.

So let me share some great news! It *is* possible to keep drama out of your workplace, and you can be the leader of this great accomplishment. You can impact an entire environment to be drama free if you are willing to pull out some courage and put the following tools in place. The first step is to identify when it is happening and the cause, and then use these simple tools and practices to avoid getting sucked in. Here's what you do.

Establish a "No Pairing" Policy.

First, encourage your employer to establish a "no pairing" policy in your workplace. This is a policy where the entire company agrees that there will be no side conversations complaining about or criticizing others who are not in the room also, unless you both are willing to be in the conversation to discuss the situation at a later time. If you are talking with your boss about something Johnny is doing that irritates you, for example, you must be willing to be in the next meeting with your boss *and Johnny*, where you share directly with Johnny how he is frustrating you. If you aren't willing to do that, then neither you nor your supervisor should be having the conversation, and that conversation should be handled directly between Johnny and yourself instead, without the involvement of the supervisor or any other employee. It is certainly always best to go directly to Johnny and discuss without your supervisor being needed for intervention. But sometimes the situation warrants a higher level of discussion, such as a situation impacting the entire organization. If your employer is not interested in establishing this policy, then adopt it for your own self. If you are consistent with this, you will be the last person in the office to be pulled into drama, and the most respected. Yes, you may be out of the loop of the juicy happenings in the office, but take that as a compliment.

Help the rescuer direct the victim to solve their own problems.

The best way to reduce drama in the workplace is to identify the drama-causing roles your coworkers play, intentional or not. Identify those who typically play the role of the rescuer, victim, or persecutor. Some may also play one role with peers and another with their supervisor. For example, an employee may play a rescuer with their peers and listen to whining from coworkers and a victim with their supervisor, spreading frustrations with others in the office about their supervisor. Know that not every employee necessarily plays one of these roles. You hopefully have some employees who have figured this out and don't play any of the three roles. If so, look to them as role models and accountability partners to lead these efforts. It is truly possible to have a drama-free life inside of work and out if you refuse to play one of these three roles.

Now it's time to put new tools in place. Here are the steps to follow to create a No Drama Zone. We are going to go to work on tools for the rescuers first.

Step One: As rescuers, train your brain to **no longer give advice** to any victim when they play the victim card. Teach them to solve their own problems. Change your messaging to ask questions only.

Step Two: Practice questions that start with "what" and include the word "you" in them. The reason for this is "what" is an action or thought-provoking start. Unlike "why," "what" is non-judgmental, so the victim becomes less defensive with this process. It makes them stop and think. The reason "you" is recommended is because it focuses the victim solely on their own part. If you use "I," then you run a high risk of owning the problem and it becomes very difficult to avoid giving advice after this, because you asked for it. Examples of good questions to direct the victim to solve their own problems include the following:

- What is your solution to the problem, if you had the power to influence the decision?
- What can you do to communicate differently, so you are not misunderstood?
- What will you say to her the next time she overreacts to the situation?

- What can you do or say to show you are not willing to be used anymore?
- What can you do to explain to your boss that they aren't being fair to you?
- What can you do to handle your frustration differently?
- What are you looking to get from me that would help you to take action?
- What is the root cause of the situation that is bothering you?
- What could you do to change their perception of you?
- What should you do to get yourself out of this undesirable situation?
- What can you do so you do not become a victim in this situation?
- What in this situation can you personally control?
- What do you think their real intention or motivation is?
- What conversation still needs to take place between you and your boss?
- What can you do to better inform your coworker with how you feel?
- What would they say the reason for the situation is if they were in the room right now?
- What do you feel your responsibility is in improving the situation?
- What could you do to show management the skills you believe you have?
- What have you done so far to leave a positive lasting impression?
- What message have your actions been speaking?
- What would you like to see happen for you to consider a positive outcome for the situation?
- What training do you need to complete to get to a higher level or to get promoted?
- What will it take for you to overcome another's objection on that project?
- What will it take for you to get over it and move on?
- What changes are you willing to make to meet that person half way?
- What do you think is something you might need more information on to better understand?
- What is one new commitment you can make to improve the situation?
- What do you think the real issue is?

- What do you need to know to make a solid educated decision?
- What part in this can you own?
- What is your motivation in taking the action you are suggesting?
- What is truly your underlying issue?
- What would be the perfect outcome if you could craft it and what can you do to get it?
- What part of the procedures are you following and what part do you still need to work on?

My recommendation is for you to think ahead of some good questions and actually write them down if you know you are going into a meeting with a victim or someone who is not taking responsibility for their actions. This really helps get the right questions asked, rather than fumbling for them in the moment.

Let's practice an example here. If you can master this concept, you will be leaps ahead of the rest of your coworkers.

Situation: Jan is upset because the last two days she has been forced to take her lunch 20 minutes late with no advance notice. Instead of going to John, who is the person she feels is the cause for this undesirable situation, she goes to Mary, a coworker in another department and vents. Mary has listened to Jan vent in the past, but has recently committed to removing herself from these venting situations going forward. So what are some good questions that Mary could ask Jan as she starts venting?

Good questions Mary should ask Jan:

- What do you know about the reason your lunch was pushed later?
- What do you think John's intentions are for making you go to lunch late?
- What could you say to John to explain how this impacts you?
- What are you looking for from me since this is not one of my employees?
- What flexibility do you have in your schedule if this appears to be needed going forward?
- What are you willing to do if it continues to be a problem after you talk to John?

- What are you willing to change in how you look at this if it becomes acceptable for John to continue being late?

Poor questions or advice by Mary:

- How can I help? (Why is this question a poor choice? Because Mary asked how she can help, and therefore sent the wrong message to Jan that Mary now owns part of this. Jan may then attempt to get Mary to solve her problem, instead of Jan owning it herself. It's better to say, "What can you do to address this with John?")

- Why don't you just go tell John's boss? (Why is this not the best advice? It might work but it has risks. Let me explain. If Jan felt comfortable going to John's boss, she would have done so already. So recognize that Jan, playing the victim role, needs some mentoring with how to go have a courageous conversation with John or his boss. Jan needs help to come up with a solution through a problem-resolution process or Mary runs the risk of owning the outcome if it doesn't go well. Jan is likely to continue to complain unless she is willing to take action and hold a conversation herself. What's risky is if Jan complains to John or his boss, and uses Mary's name in the process. This happens all too often, as victims like to build tribes. It's easier for Jan if she approaches either person and says, "Mary and I were talking and..." It would be better if Jan left Mary's office with a clear understanding that Mary is not going to fight her battles for her.)

- Why don't you just send John an email and tell him he needs to be on time? (Why is this bad advice? First, emails are never a good venue to approach or receive conflict situations or resolution demands. Second, you don't know the entire situation and it is Jan's responsibility to seek to understand why John has been late, and she should find ways to create her own solutions and understanding with face-to-face discussions, where possible. Phone is the second-best option if face-to-face is not possible.)

Note that the bullet items listed as poor questions or advice create the risk of building drama in the situation, whereas none of the questions listed as good questions run that risk. At least, it is very minimal and easily corrected if it does happen. In addition, no personal attacks are likely to fester with these good "what" questions. The conversation just naturally flows away from enabling the victim and gets them to take action instead. Just be sure to keep "you" instead of "I" in the questions, so the victim doesn't take what you say and ask you to act instead of them.

Step Three: Once you have provided the victim with some questions to solve their own problems, you must step away from the situation. The more you attempt to stay involved, the riskier it is that drama will flare up or the hard work you have done with the victim will not stick. Take great caution here. For rescuer types, once you set the tone that you are there only to ask questions to get them to think on a more global approach, and to equip the victim to solve their own problems, do not let your curiosity get the best of you and circle back with the victim later to find out what happened, how it went, or how they are feeling. Give them space to think about it, own how they handled it, and work it out themselves. Oftentimes, the venting session can be shut down nicely, but then curiosity sets in with how the meeting went with their boss, for example, and a follow-up conversation starts it up all over again. It can cause the pot to keep boiling. Do your best to stop the drama stream from churning. Let the victim continue to build their skills through addressing the situation directly with those involved if follow-up discussions are needed.

Know that drama is a choice. It only occurs when two people engage in the roles of persecutor, rescuer, or victim. It only takes two of these to cause drama. It's easy if you understand the three elements of the roles that employees might play. Using the "what" questions will be the easiest way to transition you or others out of drama. Know you must equip yourself and be on guard at all times when someone may be pulling you in. If you realize you are in the middle of the conversation and it is turning to the creation of drama, simply state your efforts to stay out of the drama zone and the messenger will typically remove themselves fairly quickly.

Lastly, sit back and watch the respect for you build as you put these practices into play to prevent drama. Enjoy the new peace and joy in finding the pleasure in your job, and watch your teammates' accountability increase as they are forced to either take action or shut up. Trust will begin building instantly.

Don't feed drama created from false accusations with more drama.

So what do you do when someone falsely accuses you of something? This is an item that is often not discussed, and certainly a trigger for gossip is when you learn that someone has gossiped about you with false accusations. To handle this takes courage, confidence, and stamina.

Unfortunately, the world includes individuals that, for reasons we will never fully understand, go on a personal attack and falsely accuse people of things that are simply not true. They exaggerate their pain, dislikes, and situations around them and attempt to create a dramatic emotional story and description of events. As they build their story, it becomes more colorful and continues to grow in their minds each time they share it. I see this really take shape on many employees' way out the door, a passive-aggressive approach to filling their soul to justify their decision to leave. It's easier if they can blame the employer for their exit rather than their own poor performance or poor job choice. And some take it to great lengths and fire off nasty letters to the HR department, management, or the board of directors.

In my experience, it is best to step back from the situation when you believe this has happened and attempt to understand the potential reasons for their behavior. When you are under attack, it is important to ensure that you stay calm and fully assess the situation. Sort out the facts from the fiction. Own the facts. Fully own them. Imagine a pin cushion full of colorful pins, where most of the pins were stabbed into the pin cushion by a hurting person to represent their entire story. That person started with a few pin facts that eventually were massaged with misinterpretation and manipulation to begin building their pin cushion, their story. Slowly, more and more pins are added to fill the pin cushion to make the story feel more real and full by the so-called victim. Unfortunately, many of the pins don't belong in the cushion if you break them down one pin at a time, and pull them out if backed up by facts. Take the approach of honestly identifying which pins are true and were justified to be placed in the pin cushion, as it will help assess why a person would take those few pins and then add more that represent the untruths. However, you will make yourself crazy if you attempt to understand something that is caused by a mental illness or hidden agendas, so don't spend too much effort or time on this. But I do recommend you spend a little effort and look for some hidden gems that might be helpful that show your blind spots or a different valuable perspective. Understanding the potential motive or coping mechanisms of the enemy can provide peace in your own mind and help you avoid becoming obsessed trying to add logic to something that is illogical. Some of the reasons people attack could be the following:

- If they make you look bad, they feel it makes them look better.
- They are incapable of admitting their imperfections. Some refer to this as narcissism.
- If they turn the attention on how you have harmed them, they feel it justifies their own poor decisions and behavior, even if not true.
- They thrive on living in a victim world.
- The more they dramatize and exaggerate the situation, the more secure they will feel about someone believing their story.
- They have an innate ability to create their own stories and then believe them.
- Their perception is formed by their inability to perceive situations from a global view, and often includes their own shortfall of being able to see a situation from a broad view and not a narrow self-centered scope.
- Selfish personal financial gain, such as the creation of a lawsuit claim, for example.
- They are jealous. Oftentimes, people gossip about you because you have something they want. Seldom are those who falsely gossip about you the ones leading out in front of you with success. They are typically less successful and following behind you.
- They create stories to cover up their own cowardly approach, using passive-aggressive tendencies to communicate. These are the ones who fire off nasty letters and emails instead of asking for a meeting to discuss.
- If they are leaving your company because of a poor career choice, it's easier to tell the world how bad you are because then their poor decision gets masked in their mind.
- They simply lack self-awareness.
- Hurt people hurt people.

In my career, I have been the victim of a select few unfortunate blatant lies against my character or some situation I was privy to. It happens. Especially as a CEO, every day I make a decision that someone is not going to like or agree with. My goal is that 99% of the decisions I make will make sense and are understood by those affected. Think about it: If I make a decision to manage a budget efficiently, someone wishes I would spend more money, give larger pay raises, or give more promotional pricing to customers. If I make a decision to expand into a new area, someone is jealous I didn't choose to expand into their area first. If I make a pricing adjustment, a customer or competitor may not approve of the decision, but management does. If I hire an employee who lacks the proven skill and I see potential, but then they don't perform, they may be disheartened that I put them in that role. So I realize I will always be under some type of judgment, which leads to personal attacks by those incapable of understanding the full situation and the facts that went into that decision, or their own responsibility.

Let me share one painful personal story with you, but know there can be others, and you must have the courage to not let these destroy you. It will illustrate the importance of staying diligent in protecting your brand when these situations creep into your life, and to stay true to who you are and what your values are. Protecting your personal brand takes courage.

Years ago, I worked alongside a talented peer executive (let's call her Victoria). Victoria was liked by some in the company and industry, although she showed signs of jealousy and an inability to accept criticism, which led to retaliation by her at times. One day, I was pulled into a situation where one of her employees expressed a meltdown of frustration with Victoria's leadership style. I immediately went into action to mentor this disgruntled employee who felt betrayed, and my advice guided them to appropriately communicate directly with Victoria and express how they felt. I advised they take a break and remove their emotions, because Victoria deserved a respectful follow-up conversation. The situation blew up quickly because Victoria observed my involvement as threatening, and immediately went into attack mode because of her false assumptions around my intent. It escalated within hours (unbeknownst to me), and she was terminated by the CEO the next day.

For years, and even to this day, Victoria continues to spread rumors in an attempt to attack my credibility and intentions. She works for a competitor and is obsessed with attempting to damage my personal brand. I immediately began to hear the stories she created, and felt the pain as some of my peers seemed to distance themselves from me. It became difficult, but I chose to simply not respond, keep my boss informed, and keep focused on my job. Over the past several years, it continues to creep into my life through work acquaintances, vendors, joint projects, and friends. In fact, I was on a plane three years after this situation, and a peer in the industry shared the rumors from Victoria that he had heard. The gist of the story created in Victoria's mind and shared publicly many times now is far from the truth. Her perception of my intentions and actions that day were simply not true.

My CEO gave me sound advice during that storm, which I will never forget. He said, "Keep doing what you are doing, and think less of her and the people who are repeating her gossip." It was great advice. I have remained friendly and kind—Victoria and I interact on occasion—and what I learned is that being on the defensive about this situation does no one any good. I simply correct the deceptive lies and fictional statements with facts when I hear them, but find ways to get away from the conversation quickly. Am I perfect every time? No. But I stay focused on acceptance and forgiveness. So why do I share this story? To illustrate that sometimes, even though you do everything right, you will still have enemies. I felt that day that encouraging her employee to address the situation and give Victoria a chance to talk through the situation was the right thing to do, and I still believe this today. You must rely on your own values. Although it is extremely difficult when Victoria's false accusations keep resurfacing today, I have chosen not to retaliate. It is Victoria's behavior to own, not mine. It was her actions that caused the separation, not mine. Her story and actions will follow her in her career and personal conscience, and mine will follow in my own. I can hold my head high when I enter a room in her presence, even though the pain is still there.

5: Use Your Employer's Resources Wisely

One of the traits that any owner or CEO appreciates in their employees is the ability to respect the resources of the company, and their commitment to use them wisely. Know that employees who treat the company's resources as treasures of their own will make better decisions for the good of the whole, and will gain respect and confidence that they will do the same if promoted in their careers with that same employer.

After all, why do most companies exist? They exist to make a profit, or to earn enough revenue to serve others if a non-profit. Either requires a wise use of resources. If you make poor financial decisions and waste company resources, it will be risky for the boss to promote you, because you will likely do the same in other areas, only at a greater level as you take on more responsibilities. Leaders want someone who is going to support the company goals and objectives, which can be significantly affected by ensuring responsible decisions around an annual budget and sound fiscal responsibility.

Quick Sabotage Assessment: Do you treat your employer's resources and assets wisely?

CAREER BUILDING CHARACTERISTICS	Y/N	CAREER SABOTAGING CHARACTERISTICS	Y/N
Do I responsibly say "no" to purchases of equipment or supplies when they are not really needed? Do I do what I can to avoid any waste in my company?		*Do I purchase excess supplies, waste product, or be sloppy with inventory items? Am I careless with internal controls to protect unpaid-for inventory walking out the door?*	

(Quick Sabotage Assessment, Cont.)

CAREER BUILDING CHARACTERISTICS	Y/N	CAREER SABOTAGING CHARACTERISTICS	Y/N
Do I respect and protect the financial resources in the company as being important to my employer, not me personally? Do I respect the decisions made by the leaders that support being cost effective?		*Do I make spending decisions at work more liberally because it's not really my money? Do I get frustrated that limits are placed on my spending and expenses?*	
Am I completely honest with whether the company really needs to spend what I am proposing? Am I willing to compromise to make the best financial decision for the company?		*Do I find ways to justify the added expense when the company would be better off not incurring the expense? Is it REALLY needed?*	
Do I get a personal fulfillment and show a buy-in of the company's profitability success?		*Do I show resentment and sarcasm towards the desire to increase profits and reinvest back into the company or pay out to shareholders or owners?*	
Do I do what is in my control to avoid overtime or unnecessary employee costs?		*Do I pad my paycheck with overtime, even if just a little, to increase my pay slightly, because no one will complain?*	
Do I support the company's pricing strategy with customers to increase net profits while balancing sales strategies? Do I do my best to honor the customer prices expected within my company? Would my boss agree with my pricing decisions as supporting the direction intended for the company?		*Do I give unnecessary discounts because it will be easy to get the sale? Do I undercut some pricing that isn't necessary? Do I make decisions on sales that cause the company to lose some of their net profit?*	

(Quick Sabotage Assessment, Cont.)

CAREER BUILDING CHARACTERISTICS	Y/N	CAREER SABOTAGING CHARACTERISTICS	Y/N
Do I travel only when necessary, or as economically possible when on business? Do I prevent any unnecessary expenses, such as meals and mileage, and spend my company's resources as if I am protecting my company's limited assets? Do I fully appreciate the opportunity to travel on business and return with knowledge justified from the investment in resources and my time away from work?		*Do I incur extra perks and meals because the company is paying for it? Do I eat a little more frivolously when I am eating on the company's dime? Do I stay in hotels that are nicer than I would normally stay in when I travel personally? Do I take a cab when travelling on business when I usually use Uber for personal transportation? When I attend a conference, do I find a few sessions where I can slip away and explore the city, and do I take a shortcut with my attendance?*	
Do I avoid the temptation of splurging on things I wouldn't normally splurge on, just because it isn't my personal money?		*Am I more willing to splurge on things, even though I know I wouldn't buy into it if it were coming out of my wallet?*	
Am I careful not to take company supplies home for personal use, such as pens, paper products, or ink cartridges?		*Do I slip some supplies in my pocket or purse because the company will never miss them and has a big supply?*	

(Quick Sabotage Assessment, Cont.)

CAREER BUILDING CHARACTERISTICS	Y/N	CAREER SABOTAGING CHARACTERISTICS	Y/N
Do I proactively manage my staffing structure, manage my team's time on the clock, and wages to prevent overtime and excess staffing expense when possible?		Do I maintain extra staff to make my life easier when the workload doesn't justify it? Am I careless with my time and slip in a little overtime occasionally or keep excess staff so days will be easier on sick days? Do I approve wage increases that are not necessary or truly earned?	

Every employee has a responsibility within their own circle to support the company financially. Even non-profit organizations that exist for the mission of a charitable organization must be fiscally responsible.

It is just as important for employees to make strong financial decisions, those which would be approved by the owners and management. Make decisions your superiors would agree with.

Know that you are not always going to make the same exact decision that the owner or CEO would have made when making financial decisions, but as long as you act in a fiduciarily responsible manner, you will be respected. You know what they would view as wasteful, impulsive, or excessive. What you want to avoid is spending money simply because you can, because it is within your authority, or simply because it is in the budget.

Use budget as a framework, not a decision model.

I'm a huge supporter of having a strategic plan and a budget. What is important is that you are careful about using the budget as a decision model to justify an unnecessary expenditure. If it's in the budget, that is step one. Step two now includes research and analysis to determine if the expense or change fits the strategic plan and serves the mission of the organization, while using resources wisely. Just because it is in the budget doesn't mean it should be spent. We see this often in government spending where the employees feel that if they don't spend the funds, they will lose the opportunity for access to the expense the following year. They then make poor decisions and spend frivolously when it is not needed.

Employees do this on occasion as well, and they can lose respect because of it. It's important that if you know there is excess in the budget, it doesn't mean you must spend that money. If you personally saved a little money in a pay period, it doesn't mean you should frivolously spend it now. You will gain great respect as a leader if you learn to make good financial decisions based on how it contributes to the success of the organization's growth, profitability, and in helping to build reserves. But if you look to the company resources as yours to distribute and spend based on your personal biases, such as purchasing a Rolls Royce when a Ford would do the job just fine, you are rapidly risking your trust level with the CEO or leadership.

Utilize the conservative approach as a safe default in spending decisions.

Be conservative. Spend what is needed but prevent excess with fancy models or unnecessary spending. If it makes sense to bring in proportionately more business, for example, then find a way to financially make the commitment. Avoid going into debt or spending if the funds aren't available. Use personal discipline when making financial decisions within your company, and it should be stronger, not weaker, than your personal discipline with your own personal finances. Let the boss determine how far out of the box they want the spending to drift if you want a liberal spending plan.

Manage personnel expenses wisely. The single largest expense for most businesses is compensation and benefit expense. Therefore, think about the value your employer is getting out of the hours you and your employees are on the clock. Work ethic includes working hard the entire time you are on the clock. But if you feel you want to slack a little, or do the "minimum" because your boss is out or no one will notice, you are not managing your company's resources wisely. Be observant and take it seriously if you are a supervisor and responsible for managing your department's personnel costs. If volume declines, for example, you should be proactive and reduce hours or shift the workload without your boss bringing it your attention. Work ethic that includes diligent watchfulness to ensure you and your team's time is used wisely will gain you respect that will give you not only the ice cream in a sundae, but the whipped cream on top. It's shameful to never get to taste the whipped cream in your career because of personal calls, tardiness, or wasted time by you or your team members.

Own providing value to your company the entire time you are clocked in. It's the largest expense that your company relies on you to manage with integrity. Practically speaking, know your and your employees' salaries in 10-minute intervals. Once you know this, ask yourself if you took that amount and put it on the table, could you honestly say you gave that much back to the company in that 10 minutes? If you and another employee just chatted for 10 minutes while on the clock, you should be able to articulate that cost to the organization. If you have an employee working overtime, you should be able to take that total cost and articulate the value you received by them working late. Is it commensurate with the outflow of cash? Of course, I'm not proposing that you become an aggressive time monster, but if you want to build your career, you will embrace this concept to help your organization be successful financially. All good employees who care even a little about improving and protecting the financial resources of their employer will make a positive impression. But complete carelessness, or knowing you are spending more than needed, will harm you for months to come if your boss can't trust your financial decisions. Be very careful you don't put your personal preferences about spending ahead of your boss's preferences. If you don't need it, don't buy it. If you can work smarter to cut hours in your department, do it.

6: Support Your Boss

Don't do things that sabotage your boss. It's that plain and simple. Find ways to support your boss, not be destructive to or about them. If you want to put the biggest roadblock in place while growing your career, outside of choosing illegal or unethical behavior, attack and criticize your boss. I shared in Chapter Two what to do if your boss is less than ethical or simply has a serious unhealthy political or self-serving agenda. For the purpose of this chapter, let's assume your boss does have your company's best interest at heart the majority of the time, even though they may lack leadership, style, or technical expertise to be a perfect boss.

Complete the self-assessment below. Many times, you may not recognize you are actually causing your boss harm with your actions, so let's talk about some self-destructive behaviors when it comes to growing your career, as it relates to how you communicate and treat your boss. These questions equally apply to your boss's boss and generally all the superiors in your organization. Included in this chapter are more thoughts that relate to any leadership position in your company, not just your direct supervisor. Don't stab them in the back!

Quick Sabotage Assessment: Do I consistently support the boss?

CAREER BUILDING CHARACTERISTICS	Y/N	CAREER SABOTAGING CHARACTERISTICS	Y/N
Do I bring ideas and thoughts to my boss and discuss how they might help them and the company to become more successful?		*Do I talk about my boss behind their back on issues, while not being willing to talk to them in person?*	

(Quick Sabotage Assessment, Cont.)

CAREER BUILDING CHARACTERISTICS	Y/N	CAREER SABOTAGING CHARACTERISTICS	Y/N
Do I consistently make decisions that I know are supportive of the company mission?		*Do I take chances here and there, even while knowing my decisions do not support the company mission, culture, or standards?*	
Do I keep my boss informed of my personal needs and performance?		*Do I sugar-coat or keep silent about my needs or cover up my mistakes, leading to a surprise when they get exposed?*	
Do I give grace on occasion to my boss, knowing they are growing in their own career and experience as well?		*Do I expect my boss to be perfect?*	
Do I support my boss with the same voice as they would use when presented an opportunity to discuss a difference of opinion or change for the company?		*Do I join in on others' dissatisfactions about my boss and/or remain silent instead of sharing my own supportive thoughts, even if I disagree?*	
Do I publicly lift my boss up?		*Do I publicly share my frustrations or challenges I have with his/her style or expertise?*	
Do I willingly coach and mentor my boss on areas that might be a blind spot for them in a caring and supportive manner?		*Do I attack or criticize my boss because they do things differently, and then spread the critical opinions, participating in a destructive gossip chain?*	
Do I take the responsibility for my own actions?		*Do I blame my boss for something they did wrong as the reason for my poor performance or mistake?*	

(Quick Sabotage Assessment, Cont.)

CAREER BUILDING CHARACTERISTICS	Y/N	CAREER SABOTAGING CHARACTERISTICS	Y/N
Do I alert my boss of areas of potential concern?		Do I stay quiet and let the boss take the brunt of it and have them be surprised when it comes to light?	
Am I loyal to my boss and contribute to their continued success?		Do I find ways to express they are not the right person for the job, and contribute to making their success more difficult?	

Plainly stated, your boss deserves your support and honesty, even if it means an uncomfortable conversation with them on occasion. Hopefully, you have a boss who welcomes your ideas when offered with care and concern for the betterment of the team and their success. Your boss is responsible to lead your team, so the more information they have to work with, the better things will flow and the more successful your company will be.

It's likely your boss has many responsibilities and is juggling many hats, so understanding and helping when one of those hats might fall to the floor is a great start. Ask yourself how you can pick that hat up and offer some assistance, rather than stomp on it or walk off, leaving it on the floor. Is there a deadline approaching that they may have forgotten about that you can help your boss meet? Is data being gathered for a report that is not yet available that you can proactively help create? Did you observe a potential scheduling conflict coming up for a holiday that they may not be aware of, and then take the initiative to fix it? Can you simply offer to take one thing off their desk that you are capable of handling? The worst thing you can do is share with others where you see your boss missing an important detail, such as filing an important tax document, and not proactively grab it from the office and get your boss's attention with a helpful attitude. Never make your boss feel bad because of an oversight on their part. They'll sense it quickly, breaking down trust and questioning which side you are on, the company's or, selfishly, yours.

There are several specific behaviors you can embrace and choices you can make that send a strong message that you are there to be part of the success of your boss and your organization. Let me break down a few these in greater detail.

Make decisions that support your boss's direction.

You will find more insight in Chapter Seven about understanding the mission, while supporting your organization and boss in their work towards fulfilling that mission. In this section, I'll share another important factor regarding the actual decisions you make while working in the organization. Everyone has a different level of autonomy with decisions, and that autonomy is typically granted as you build the trust of management in the organization. It is important that you never discount the importance of knowing, with confidence, that you understand your boss's direction and you *know* that your decisions would be supported. I'm not saying that you need to, or should, run all decisions by them—quite the contrary. But are you confident they would agree with and support your actions if you asked? It's a good gut check to complete on occasion. Of course, there will always be some gray areas for those decisions that you need to have further training or discussions on, but if you set a personal goal to understand your boss's preferences and company guidelines, you'll make better, well-rounded decisions that will naturally fall into place with your boss's approval and the company mission.

So how do you earn the level of trust that leads to empowerment to make consistent decisions you know would be in unison with your boss's responsibilities? And how do you do this safely? First and foremost, you must ask questions if you have any doubt of the policies and procedures, even if not written and simply expected to be understood. If you know the standard procedure is to obtain a signature on a purchase order, for example, take the initiative to identify when an exception would be acceptable by asking questions during training or normal processing. Do this before the need for the exception actually occurs, so you are prepared to make the right decision in the unusual moment. Identify the red flags and pay close attention to them. If you have decisions you are ready to make that you know your boss would not support, you must stop, regroup, and start over with your decision process. If you don't, you put your career at risk, and these typical incidents are not worth the potential negative outcomes when/if they rise to the surface at a later date.

Be very careful you don't get hung up on stubbornness here. Examples of this might include a questionable expenditure that could easily be buried in a larger purchase order that you know your boss might take issue with. Or maybe it might include a decision to provide a discount to a client that you know doesn't support your company's pricing objectives. Or it might be that without approval, you intentionally allow your employees to work different hours than what the personnel policy states, knowing your boss would object if they were aware. Justifying deception—because it will make your life easier, because you want more control, or because it will cause you to be liked more by your team—will lead you down a dangerous slope to ski on. It may allow you to get your project done sooner or make life easier in the moment, but the work that you may have to put in to correct the damage of distrust in the future is far greater than following the direction your boss lays out for you. It may even cause irreparable damage. Many times, employees bypass safety standards established by top management, which can eventually lead to an accident or a violation of a regulatory requirement that is identified in an audit. These situations do not set your boss up for success. Complete the gut check often and ask yourself, "Is this the same decision my boss would support?" Their success often contributes to your success.

My recommendation is to invest more effort in how to overcome objections and discuss differences in opinions than taking the risk of doing it your way when you know it won't be supported or goes against company policy. I've seen so many great employees sabotage their careers because they took shortcuts that would make their boss cringe, become stubborn about their personal preferences, make exceptions they know will cost the company money, or put the employees or company at risk. You get paid to complete a job according to company guidelines, so making decisions contrary to your boss's expectations will set you up for a less-than-positive result.

So how do you work through the different opinions or obstacles that creep into the workplace from time to time? The first step is to gain a good perspective on the reason you might choose a direction different from the boss's intended instruction or the company's mission. Below are some examples of tactics that employees create in their own minds as justifications that lead to poor choices, and you can certainly add your own. Step one is identifying them, becoming keenly aware when they creep in, and then working to recognize why you might think this way and what situations trigger your temptation to be contrary to your boss's direction. Here are a few really poor justification statements that can backfire and sabotage your career:

- It makes the job more difficult.
- It's a stupid policy anyway.
- I believe there is an easier way, and the policy doesn't really matter.
- It seems like a waste of time.
- My employees deserve more.
- I just don't want to deal with it.
- The boss has no clue how this works.
- The boss just doesn't understand.
- I have more expertise in this area than my boss.
- The boss will never know.
- The boss gets paid the big bucks, so let them own it if it goes bad.
- It doesn't really matter.
- My boss is out of touch and doesn't understand how it works anyway.
- I don't want to cause any friction in my department between management and my team, so we'll just let it be.
- I work hard.
- I deserve this.
- I don't want to admit we made a mistake.

If any of these statements resonate with you, it's important to dig deep and assess why. What's your coping mechanism when you don't get your way in a decision process? Find some opportunities to discuss these with your boss, but also respect where the company is coming from. Know that you may tend to create these justifications in your own mind, and immediately it may cause you to put stones, and sometimes boulders, in the road to your success, especially when you know they wouldn't be supported by your boss, the company manual, or potentially even the law. Identify why you think these statements or thoughts may be tempting to use and get some help with your own list first, or it will follow you to the next job and continue to creep in as an obstacle in your career. Some reasons you could be having these thoughts might include the following:

- Ego, arrogance, or pride; the desire to be and know more than your boss
- Lack of knowledge or expertise
- Impatience
- Lack of self confidence
- Lack of ownership
- Fear of difficult conversations
- Dishonesty
- Self-centeredness
- Dislike of authority
- Fear of failure
- Distrust
- Control
- Perfectionism
- Codependence
- Difference in desired service standards; quantity vs. quality preferences
- Lack of understanding of approval process

These are only some of the reasons employees choose to go a different direction than their bosses, and if any of these resonated with you, talk it out with someone you trust. Identify your triggers. Then go to work on them and create action plans to tackle your triggers with courage when needed. Many companies have employee assistance programs, or even a trusted friend or professional counselor can help. Select someone who won't judge you, but will tell you what you need to hear. Select someone who also understands the importance of this topic in building trust and your career.

Integrity, or a lack thereof, almost always shows up, good or bad. It's critical to build a continuous growth strategy in your career and be proud of what you have accomplished. You do this by making decisions you know are in the best interest of your boss and would be supported by them. Never discount that your coworkers also observe your decisions and every move. It could even be that one of your coworkers may become your boss someday. If you stay in the same industry or live in a small community, it is not uncommon that a current coworker or boss will be a future coworker or boss in a different company someday.

It's important your current and future bosses trust your commitment to the company policies and values. A conflicting decision today might even rise to the surface well after you leave the company someday, and it will rest on your personal shoulders as a negative impact to your brand forever. Yes, some things may go unnoticed, but overall, the pieces that lead to you completing the responsibilities assigned to you and how you go about doing them correctly involve many choices and decisions that all roll up into supporting your performance for the company. Are yours in sync with your boss?

Keep your boss informed of your unique needs.

We are all unique and different. It is important to openly discuss your unique needs with your boss. There is no reason to be embarrassed or shy away from expressing what is important to you. In fact, it is critical you do so, especially if your demand or needs expressed are going to cause any resentment on your part while you are supporting the company and/or your boss. If you don't give your boss the opportunity to better understand how your position at the company can be mutually beneficial to the both of you, you likely will be at a disadvantage in growing your career.

Each of us also has personal needs and preferences that are important to us individually and in our career. This can include preferences such as flexibility in our schedule, a quiet work environment, or a certain pay level and benefit offering. It could be the difference in how you like to receive recognition, the need for time to process big decisions, or how you like to learn (i.e. verbal vs. visual). None are right or wrong, unless they are a mismatch between what you will accept and what your company can offer. What is important is that you know you have the responsibility to identify these, rate them in order of importance and tolerance level, and then communicate with your boss.

The ideal time to be open and honest about your preferences or needs is in your job interview or before you accept the position. It's not sufficient or appropriate to simply land the job, then go to work on your non-negotiables after you start employment. If you determine a certain need is non-negotiable and important to you, it certainly should be discussed before you accept the position. Note that saving this until you get the job offer could end up being okay, but ignoring it until you are on the payroll is not. It can create a distrust right at the outset of your employment if you do so later on. If it is not a good match, it's better that you don't try to put a square peg in a round hole.

So let's talk about a few non-negotiables and how you might handle these appropriately, because this can be tricky at times. The rate of pay might be one of them. If you truly need a certain salary to pay your bills and you cannot work for less, then it should be presented as a clear non-negotiable for you when that becomes the case. That might be prior to accepting the position, or later on when your personal needs change. Simply present your needs, but don't take it personally if the company cannot meet your needs. Instead, discuss a good compromise strategy so the conversation creates a professional experience while matching needs to wants for both parties: you and your organization. Your employer has limitations they must work within, such as a budget, goals, strategic plan, and a growth strategy. Give the company time to take your requests and evaluate how they might fit their needs with yours, while also building your request into their policies for consistency among the organization.

Another example of a non-negotiable need you might have is if your family requires a certain type of medical insurance and you cannot get coverage elsewhere. You may also have preferences around the logistics of your work environment, such as steering clear of areas that cause allergic reactions or other areas where physical limitations might exist, such as the inability to climb stairs. And what about commute requirements or schedule to pick up children from daycare?

Make a list of the preferences and the non-negotiable needs. The creation of your non-negotiable list will simply contain the things you will say no to a job offer for if they aren't provided. Be careful here and don't lump general preferences in this list that truly don't belong on the non-negotiable list. Be honest with yourself about the importance of preferences and needs to you. Be clear about the level of preference when discussing these needs with your boss, such as the acceptable time you will wait for your needs to be met. If a preference is presented incorrectly or impatiently, it may cause your employer to make a decision that is not in your best interest in order to attempt to satisfy a component of your request. It is important to know that it doesn't make you a bad person or a poor employee if you are performing your job duties well and simply have a unique preference, but it isn't appropriate to accept a job and then bring it into the discussion as a "must-have" later on. That simply puts your boss or hiring manager in a bad position and hurts your reputation and the trust in you and/or your personal motivations. The boss may ask themselves, "What else are they going to spring on me later?" The boss may also have some concern with how they might be manipulated by you in the future with new demands, so be careful here, while being honest with yourself and the sacrifices you are willing to make. You don't want to put your boss on guard for future requests, which might put a strain in your relationship, so appropriate timing and clear expectations in these discussions is important.

You have choices in life, and one of those important choices for most people is where you work. The primary context of writing this book is to share my experience with seeing employees make choices that help or hurt their career: They may choose to stick with a position that pays off in the long run, helping their career, or they may abandon ship too quickly for a new position, because they are being short-sighted with how they assess the pros and cons. The latter is a result of making short-term decisions based on simple preferences, which can be detrimental to their career. Instead, you should make strategic, career-building moves with the big picture in mind.

Although this section in this chapter is about informing your boss of your preferences, it really means to talk to your boss and discuss acceptable options for your non-negotiable and negotiable preferences. It is essential to know what is truly important to you during this process. List what is negotiable and what is not in your career and job requirements. Don't play games here, and even more importantly, don't communicate your needs with bratty ultimatums. If you want to move to another department because you don't like a coworker, for example, don't aggressively demand your boss to make the change now or you'll quit. They might just take your threat and accept it. After all, who wants an employee on their team that exhibits such immature behavior?

Occasionally, I see employees make the decision to move onto another company because they have a particular preference with their current position, such as hours or locations where they work, and these needs have not yet been discussed with the boss. Unfortunately, these are often shared for the first time in an exit interview or with a coworker. Even worse, they are dropped as a hint in the hallway weeks before and then they wonder why their importance wasn't seriously picked up on by management. Your career is an investment, so why wouldn't you strategically arrange and plan out your needs conversation carefully and give both parties the opportunity to create a mutually beneficial arrangement? It is frustrating to the leader of a company, for example, when a part-time employee leaves because they wanted full-time hours, but they refused to discuss the possibility of that need becoming a reality in their current position.

It's simply short-sighted to make career moves based on a particular unmet need or preference that was never discussed, when it may in fact be a negotiable item. If you avoid this professional discussion with your boss, you inevitably set yourself up for a poor decision or risky obstacle in your career. And don't make assumptions on how they will respond. You and your career are worth the discussion about your needs with your boss. Don't make this crucial mistake and diminish the value of the conversation that will verify if your needs can be met. And never make a career change based only on assumptions because you don't want to have an uncomfortable conversation. Never.

Now let's talk about the negotiables where you have flexibility in your position. Each person has areas of preferences that are more flexible in nature. These are areas you express or share with your boss, and you are clear about what your willingness level to negotiate is. For example, if you are willing to commute to a branch several miles away until another opportunity opens up at a closer location, that preference would fall into this category. Your boss should know your preference and you should have an open discussion about the possibility of future considerations, not a demand or guarantee of specifics at this stage in the game. When your boss provides that coaching time where a general discussion is appropriate around how you are feeling about your job, this is a great time to politely and respectfully bring it up. Share honestly how you feel about the importance of what your needs and preferences are. But also be open-minded that the boss may be unable to accommodate your request, and that it's not a personal issue. No boss likes to deliver news that you don't want to hear, so be selective with what exceptions are important enough for you that you want to bring to the table, and never carry a grudge if you don't get your way.

Also, if your employer has certain restrictions explained to you when you accept the position, such as the requirement you must stay in your position for one year before applying for a promotion or move within the company, honor that requirement. You knew what it was when you accepted the position. Respect it, even if you don't like it. Feel free to share your desire and interest with your next move, but don't make a request contrary to your previous agreement.

So how do you handle the rejection or refusal by your boss to honor an unusual request made by you? Let me first say I have seen talented employees misstep here because they take the decision personally and with a closed mind. They only thought about themselves and how it impacted them. Don't do this. Your boss's number one loyalty is to the company and the policies and structure already put in place. They have to be able to sleep at night believing in their decisions. The best way to handle this is to thank them for the consideration and express your appreciation that it was at least considered. Be ever so grateful for this. Then walk away and never bring it up again, especially if you have distaste in your mouth around the decision. Most critically, don't share with any team members or gossip about your rejected personal request and whether it was honored or not, unless you have facts that discrimination or some other type of unethical behavior is taking place.

Also, never discuss with others to build your case of unfair favoritism. Each person's situation is very different, and much of it is personal and shouldn't be discussed with others. You will likely deliver only one part, *your* part, of the story when you do this. If you are on the receiving end of this type of discussion with a coworker, avoid the conversation and direct them back to their supervisor to discuss further, as your involvement will only taint your judgment in how you interpret the situation, knowing you likely aren't receiving the full story. If you carry your discontent outside your boss's office, it is destructive towards your boss and the company. There are simply areas that are intended to stay between the two of you and/or your human resources department. It is important to know when to accept and support a decision, going back to Chapter One, and when a further discussion is needed to clarify any misinformation.

Never—and I say *never*—hold a grudge that comes into your work environment because you made a special request that wasn't granted. Put yourself in the shoes of your boss and how difficult it is to keep sanity with the numerous personal requests they receive on a daily basis, that you know nothing about, and where no two situations are alike. Understand that you may be unaware of the many other requests that may be culminating with the team members that your boss is balancing as well. I personally hold a belief system that limits requests that fall outside the personnel policies to emergencies only. You will gain tremendous respect by your boss when you do this, and a confidence will be gained that if they ever need you to step in and lead a new team, you will have good judgment when you might someday start getting the same requests. Let me reinforce that how you handle your personal affairs and requests will impact how you handle your employees' affairs when you become a supervisor. This can become a roadblock for a future consideration to move you up in the company if not handled well.

This is why I highly discourage discussing your salary with other employees. It's a no-no in my opinion, and it only causes you, your peers, or your employer potential problems and could cause them to get stuck in an uncomfortable position. Your salary is based on the work you do and is between you and your boss. Complaining about your salary to other coworkers is like complaining about your boss or the leadership's decision-making skills. Not cool. You never know if a special arrangement was made to get an employee to sign onto your company, a unique situation that is promised in the future, and the like. Keep your salary highly confidential, and don't manipulate others to tell you even what their range is. Just go to work doing a good job, communicate directly with your boss about your honest needs, and the rest should fall into place. There is always someone who can find something they feel is unfair with any salary structure or unique salary package for a team member. If salaries are not published, it's each individual person's private information to own and keep confidential.

In summary, know that it is your boss's responsibility to follow the company guidelines and own them as if they were theirs to own. Never put your boss in a situation where you ask them to bend the policies established by management, especially with an ultimatum. Instead, brainstorm how to address the situation the best way you can. This may include solutions such as a leave of absence or a schedule change. Their job is difficult as they manage various employees that come to the company from completely different environments with various family dynamics, geographic areas, value systems, political views, health, faith, etc.

So how do we work with this effectively and how does a company serve all employees with so many differences? Each company starts with establishing rules, guidelines, and policies to deliver to its employees to protect them and the company, while providing a framework for employees to work within to get the job done. The larger a company, the more difficult it is to create standards that can still be flexible, while also protecting the company. Invest in understanding the policies of your organization, the benefit to the company because of their existence, and refer to them first before making any special requests. Someday, if you become a supervisor, the personnel policies will become your best friend and they will be a good guide to keep focus and order in the workplace, so get comfortable with them.

Extend grace for your boss's imperfections.

I am a huge believer that every person in the organization, clear up to the CEO, deserves grace at times. You aren't perfect. Why do you expect your boss to be? Humans have different strengths, talents, creativeness, communication styles, relationship building skills, and technical abilities. Humans have good days and bad. If you were to look at the responsibilities and stress of a CEO or senior executive, it would seem you would understand and be more forgiving of their imperfections, not less. But it doesn't typically work that way in many organizations or in the minds of employees. The minute someone earns the title of "supervisor," many instantly expect them to have it all figured out. It is such a deceiving expectation. They are people just like you and me, but with different responsibilities. Many times, they are stepping into new jobs. Yes, we often expect the CEO to be the most consistent and courageous person in the organization that has their "A" game on all the time. That is normal.

However, know that all positions—including the CEO—need mentoring and coaching at times, and every position requires training and experience in the position to perfect it. We all have blind spots and if you can graciously help the CEO or your boss see theirs, you are supporting the company and will definitely gain respect as a current or future leader. If you can master the skill of mentoring a person in the organization that is higher in the organization than you, you will become a great communicator and be much more effective when you have the opportunity to advance in the organization down the road. It will make you stronger and able to have difficult conversations. It will also earn you mounds of trust and respect as a person.

I have been blessed at times as a leader with direct reports who were willing to "coach up," as I call it. They had strong enough communication skills and cared about the organization enough to privately share with me how I might have come across during a discussion, for example, or how I tended to be the "easy button" with the answers too quickly. They needed me to let them learn and work more independently in their decision making, and they communicated this in a loving and professional manner. My employees extended grace in those situations, and I did my best to embrace it. Being open to constructive criticism is part of being an effective leader, and quite frankly, it's part of being an effective human being. These experiences only strengthened my relationship with my employees, knowing they had the courage to share something uncomfortable, and also the trust in them that their input would be received without retribution by me. I was appreciative for the heads up, and it allowed me to be more cognizant in future meetings.

By receiving this information firsthand, it was much more helpful than hearing through the grapevine. I knew if employees were willing to bring these topics to my attention firsthand, then I could imagine them being willing to have a difficult conversation with their employees in the future, which would instill confidence in the next promotion discussion where their name might be deliberately thrown in the hat. It will typically always have this effect if delivered with empathy and care. Equally so, the opposite is true. If you complain to someone else about your boss instead of going directly to them, your boss will have a hard time trusting you. Period!

The times when stepping up with communication is ineffective and doesn't work is when a messenger is sent to deliver the message on someone else's behalf. In that case, it creates distrust and a lack of confidence in those who weren't willing to bring forward the constructive criticism on their own behalf and turf. The messenger is then flagged as a gossiper leading a pack of wolves. Good leaders take constructive criticism and ponder it, and they are also willing to deliver it. I've had many times in my career where listening to uncomfortable feedback has been the best thing I could do in that situation. As a CEO, I know I have blind spots, and so does every leader. I just hope the opportunities to need grace are few and far between, and

I'm able to identify them because they have been kindly brought to my attention.

There's an unwritten and unfair rule that says, "The boss must be perceptive enough to see everything in the organization as it unfolds right before their eyes." I've seen employees place such an unreasonable standard on the leaders in an organization that they actually look for them to do something wrong. They lurk in every meeting or conversation and listen intently to seize the moment when they can gain ammunition to use against their boss, leading to the creation of ridiculous drama by being critical of the leader. They'll attack situations, such as the leader using a certain word to describe something, or become unforgiving of a missed appointment, for example. When the boss does misstep, this distasteful type of critical employee thrives on their mistake. In these situations, it is almost certain that same critical employee will never be given the chance to grow in the organization. After all, what leader in their right mind would want to promote an employee under them who would be unable to support them when they fall or have a misstep? Leaders want employees who will share in the work that needs done, and some of that work is mentoring each other for the betterment of the organization, not tearing down certain individuals because of their critical nature.

If you have a tendency to fall on the more critical side, rather than using empathy and compassion, make a commitment today to change. Start by making a list of things you are grateful for in your employer and boss. Next, make a list of what bothers you and ask what you have control over and focus only on improving those areas. And thirdly, list the areas you believe your boss would be open to learning more about to grow them as a leader, and request a meeting to chat with them during an appropriate time. The appropriateness of that meeting is important, as you must allow sufficient time to talk through the situation or feelings. It should not be done in the morning if your boss is not a morning person or has deadlines to meet every morning with reports, for example. Avoid scheduling this meeting when your boss is on their way to another meeting or showing up as a quick pop in when you know they don't do well with surprise meetings, for example, or you may set the conversation up for failure. The important part to remember is that the conversation will likely create anxiety on both of your parts, so invest the necessary time for careful communication and planning, as this may be the most important conversation you have with your boss.

I often wonder who created the next unwritten rule that states, "It's not our job to help the boss be successful." Know that if you can help your boss be successful, the power is in *your* hands. You will almost always be more successful in your own role and move up in your career at a faster pace. My employees know that I believe every person in the organization should coach down, sideways, and up! So now let's talk about how to support the boss and make them look good. By "look good," I am referring to showing up as a courageous and intelligent leader and employee who makes respected decisions, and well represents the company brand. Imagine a situation where the boss might be describing a big change that appears to cause some confusion with the team because of their choppy explanation. What might that look like when a team player instantly steps up and offers help, realizes some preparation steps are missing that could add clarity for everyone, and immediately owns it and lets the boss know they will bring it to the team for clarity soon? It is clear that particular boss will be forever grateful for the rescue gesture, teamwork, accountability from their team, and will build trust in the proactive employee who will likely have their back going forward. Finding the opportunity and seizing the moment to turn any oversight or difficult situation into a positive one for the boss is wise and impactful. Do what you can to make the boss look good when they make a mistake with appropriate actions to improve a situation.

I advise you to never put your boss up on a pedestal and expect them to be perfect. Recognize the leaders in your organization as people, and appreciate the additional responsibilities, stressful decisions, and workload they carry every day. Also recognize that being a CEO is lonely at the top, so support them along the journey. I remember when I was a VP of Finance and had a great relationship with the employees in the various branches and departments, and we talked on occasion about a variety of interests and shared in the fun events and stories. Small talk was part of the environment. Then I was promoted to CEO in that same organization with the same people, and all of a sudden, these same people became slightly tense or nervous when I entered the room. I truly was the same person, just with different responsibilities, but things still changed. Ask how you can interact differently or support your CEO or owner of your organization. It will have a positive impact on your career. People become intimidated or scared by the CEO sometimes, and the CEO can feel it. I even take all my employees out for coffee just to chat their first week and many still become intimidated when I enter a room. Give your boss and the CEO appreciation notes and tender care, as they need positive encouragement just like every other employee, but are often the last ones to receive it.

Publicly speak positively about your boss and the leadership of your company.

You will have opportunities to share publicly how you feel about your work and the current leaders of your organization. Even over dinner with friends, they may ask, "How do you like your job?" Chapter Two covers more specifically about creating your personal brand, but in this chapter, it is meaningful to point out the importance of avoiding criticizing the leaders of your company publicly. Take the opportunity as it warrants to actually lift your boss up in conversations, while never sharing their weaknesses publicly. Become intimately knowledgeable about your leader's strengths and use your circle of influence to promote them and the positive attributes they possess. By promoting the leadership of your organization, you are promoting the organization itself. This doesn't mean you need to create fictitious strengths and compliments, but every leader has some meaningful strengths that make them unique. How you talk about your boss affects the brand you create for your organization, not to mention the brand you create for yourself. And believe it or not, it does affect the profitability and business driven to your employer. After all, who wants to recommend a business that you hear negative things about from an employee experience? And never forget that more profitability can only help employee benefits and compensation packages, if you want to look at this as an added bonus.

Communities are often much smaller than we realize when it comes to people knowing people, especially in this day of social media. It is simply never a good idea to be negative about your company, and certainly about your boss, especially at networking events or in public settings. Friends talk, even when they promise they won't. If you talk negatively about your organization or its leaders, you are basically hurting the very organization that is putting food in your mouth or gas in your tank. They are your source of income and career advancement opportunities, so sabotaging them is like putting a nail in the coffin of your own career. It's difficult to take the nail out once it's been hammered in, without leaving an ugly mark. Know that no boss is going to promote someone who is hurting the organization's brand. It is a career killer, so find ways to express the positive and lift your company up. Promoting your company actually drives business in the door, and that business eventually lands in your paycheck when turned to profits. Every opinion about your organization or boss leaves an impact on the reputation of the product or service you sell. Consumers rarely separate the values and treatment of employees with the products and services companies sell. They go hand in hand. Talking positive about your company and your boss is a great, inexpensive way to use marketing tactics for great company awareness.

Be prepared when someone asks you, "Do you like your boss?" Praise where you can, and if you have issues, choose your words carefully. Be very careful with venting regularly to your close family and friends, especially with an exaggerated version. This can become an undesirable and bad habit that turns into a daily conversation, causing you to lose your positive perspective of your employment. Once I didn't hire someone I knew because he vented often about his employer, which caused me to question if he had the potential to be a satisfied employee. You never know what opportunity might open up in the future.

Years ago, I had an employee who represented consistently how satisfied she was in her job and how much she appreciated the leadership of our organization, and me as her supervisor. One day, I stumbled onto an email sent to me in error where she was bashing our organization and the leadership to her husband. The tone of the email was such that she expressed how she worked in a horrible work environment and how it was causing her extreme stress and anxiety.

I was shocked, as she always represented herself proactively as loving her job and appreciative for the opportunity. She was a great worker and I would never have guessed this email would have come from her. After visiting with her about this, she was embarrassed and humiliated. She expressed that she got attention from her husband and friends through carrying this mantra, even though she truly did not feel that way. We had a good discussion about the potential of her friends and family ever recruiting business to our employer, based on the perception she was leaving with them. Her husband worked for one of the largest local corporations and I shared with her the unlikely event that he would ever refer business, based on the discontent she was communicating. Plus, he was encouraging her to find a different job, even though she loved her current job. Talk about confusion for him. She just didn't express it honestly to him. It was a great discussion, but I can assure you it negatively impacted the trust level between us and the opportunity for a career advancement for her. She had a great career going, and this impacted her negatively in many ways. She soon left the organization and struggled to land a job in a good position after that, letting me know later that she regretted her actions.

There are many external audiences that can be impacted about the external promotion of your leadership team and company. Know that it's just as important to promote your boss and educate others about your company in a positive and genuine manner to other external audiences where capable and worthy. These audiences may include customers, family and friends, vendors, board members, volunteers, and even regulators and auditors. Each of the members in these audiences also form opinions about your organization and the leadership based on what is shared about them. Always be cautious, as it isn't unusual when your comments may go full circle and land in your boss's lap someday. Simply put, don't bash your company or its leaders, not even with your drinking buddies or best friends.

Lift your bosses up and they will likely be there to lift you up in your career someday. I can recall a few times where I have had my employees' unintended negative rants on social media or their Friday night bar talk forwarded my way from a supportive individual. There are many who will come to the boss's rescue if they hear others act unprofessionally about your company. You never want that to be things you said. You'd much rather those comments be about how positive you were about the company and how you serve your customers well.

Know that I understand difficult environments exist and I am not a believer that every organization is worthy of lifting up and promoting. I once worked in an extremely dysfunctional organization for a short stint in my career where it would have been difficult to talk positive about the leader, but I was able to understand the positive value of the mission and find opportunities to improve and promote the services they provided, regardless of the leadership. So what do you do if you have issues with your boss or company values? First and foremost, find an opportunity to courageously talk with them directly. Avoid venting to a coworker or taking it externally. I regret being less than perfect in this situation. Often, when venting occurs, what is shared has never been shared with the boss or appropriate human resource department directly. Second, find a professional trusted mentor or leadership group where confidential issue processing occurs, such as Vistage International, where what is shared in the group stays in the group. There are many of these where the group signs confidentiality agreements and acts as a good resource if you need an avenue to discuss difficult and complex situations. If you happen to occupy the role of a CEO or top executive, you will need a confidential and trusted sounding board to discuss issues, and Vistage has been a great resource for me in this area. There are others as well, and you can identify them by simply asking many of the top leaders in your community of their knowledge of strong leaders or local confidential mastermind groups. For the most part, however, most issues can easily be resolved and should be by discussing directly with your boss and bringing forth solutions internally.

7: Support and Fully Understand the Company's Mission

One of the most important investments you can make in your career is to buy into the mission of the company you work for. Treat it as if you are making a large financial investment in your company. Research the mission, study it, and be sure you find a way to fully support what you are investing in. Your career will be one of the biggest assets you acquire and build. Learn as much as you can about your company. Find out the reason for your company's existence. Learn the mission in enough detail that you feel you can fall in love with it, even if you are just dating today. Support the mission and immerse yourself in it in your everyday interactions with your organization. By not doing so, it will be easy to get off track in your own focus and where to use your skills that will have the most impact on the organization.

On the next page is a quick assessment you can take to identify how you might be doing in this area in your current job and organization today. It will also give you some things to think about and observe if you are scoping out a new position. Jot down areas of opportunity you might have to improve on to avoid sabotaging yourself unintentionally. The assessment has questions intended to guide you through various areas that might reflect your support and understanding for the company's mission.

Make it your strongest desire to understand where the captain of the ship you are aboard is headed. You are a crewmember and need to feel confident you are supporting the captain's course. You were likely hired because the leadership of the organization saw something in you and your skills that would support the desired vision and goals of the company. Do you know what those are? Never lose sight of the importance of this, as it will help solidify your progression and development opportunities in the company. Your career growth will be assisted greatly if you know not only where you are heading, but where the leadership of the organization is heading as well. Steering the ship off course, whether intentionally or inadvertently, can potentially run your career aground. The leaders of companies want to have a team of shipmates they can trust that will enthusiastically navigate, build, and support the vision they are leading, most often directed by the board of directors or the owners of the company.

Quick Sabotage Assessment: Do you build a strong belief in the vision, and support your company's mission?

CAREER BUILDING CHARACTERISTICS	Y/N	CAREER SABOTAGING CHARACTERISTICS	Y/N
Do I understand the company's mission and can I recite it? If unwritten, have I discussed the mission with the appropriate leaders to ensure I fully understand? Do I know where the mission statement is located so I can memorize it?		Am I unclear what the company's mission states? Have I chosen to become absorbed in my daily job duties and my own department and find that I don't really care what the big mission for the organization is?	
Do I understand what an ideal customer profile looks like for the company?		Do I take on a new customer opportunity without first considering whether it is a good fit with the company mission?	
Do I consistently make decisions that are supportive of the company's direction, communicated by top management?		Do I sometimes make decisions for the wrong reasons, such as serving my personal preferences, creating a quick solution, or sacrificing integrity for profitability, all contrary to the company's mission? Do I act or feel contrary to the goals of the company and resist finding a way to get on board?	

(Quick Sabotage Assessment, Cont.)

CAREER BUILDING CHARACTERISTICS	Y/N	CAREER SABOTAGING CHARACTERISTICS	Y/N
Do I know the company's competitive advantage?		*Do I lack discipline to stay focused on perfecting the competitive advantage communicated through the company mission? Do I try to be competitive in all things to all people, knowing some are contrary to the company mission?*	
Do I understand the organizational structure and who in the organization owns the creation of the mission, and how others might support and execute on the various components?		*Do I challenge or discount the intention around the mission and/or who owns the direction? Do I try to steer others to serve a different purpose than I know the company strives for?*	
Do I know how my job can truly support the mission, impacting the end product and/or customer experience?		*Am I selfish with how I approach my individual role? Do I work within my own comfortable bubble and forget I am part of the desired customer experience or corporate mission? Do I ignore how my work affects the front-line customer interaction or support thereof?*	
Are my actions in alignment with the company mission, professionally and personally?		*Are my actions out of sync with what I know the leaders and owners of the company would approve of? Do I place a careless lack of importance on every single company value stated?*	

(Quick Sabotage Assessment, Cont.)

CAREER BUILDING CHARACTERISTICS	Y/N	CAREER SABOTAGING CHARACTERISTICS	Y/N
Do I believe in what my company is doing, and do I support it publicly?		*Do I publicly criticize or discount the value of the company? Do I communicate in any manner that I don't support my company? Am I sarcastic about what the company is trying to accomplish? Do I gossip about and challenge the company's direction?*	
Do I make an effort to support the culture, a component intended to support the mission in a positive way, and professionally bring ideas forward for the betterment of the organization that also support the mission?		*Do I attempt to create my own cultural values that make my job easier or more comfortable for me? Do I keep my ideas to myself when they can help the company? Do I ignore one or more of the cultural values to selfishly suit me? Do I excuse my poor behavior?*	

One of the daily, and often unspoken, expectations as you focus on growing your career and skills within your company is to know and understand the company's mission. It's the organization's primary objective for existence and shouldn't be taken lightly. Often, we focus solely on our individual roles or tasks and we don't think about the end result of how our efforts roll up into the big audacious mission and the meaning behind it that is important to the leaders.

It's logical you were likely exposed to the company's mission during your orientation when you were hired. Or maybe it was delivered to employees at an annual staff meeting or revised at a recent strategic planning session. But when was the last time you read the mission statement, studied it word for word, and then thought about how you actually support it within your own role as an employee?

There are many ways to get the mission of the company ingrained in your mind. It doesn't matter how big or small an organization is. Most have a mission—or at least an assumed or intended mission—that is supported and driven by the owners or board of directors. I've been blessed in my career to work for organizations that are passionate about their mission, so wrapping my arms around them and understanding them fully flowed naturally for me. Even more compelling than understanding the mission, I found that truly embracing and believing in it simply came with the territory: It was a factor important enough to me that I investigated and studied the cause before I ever accepted the positions.

In fairness though, most of my career has been in the non-profit arena. I will say that employees of non-profit organizations tend to be far more bought into the mission of their organizations than those with profit-oriented organizations, but both can offer compelling missions that provide fulfilling careers. It is possible that for-profit organizations can live and breathe compelling missions, similar to non-profit organizations, if they invest in the "why" of their existence, and provide value in helping others solve a need. Non-profits do this well, as they operate in a charitable or cause-driven fashion and are often helping others. Let me share a few examples of companies I admire, whose employees believe in their mission.

Les Schwab Tires – Their tag line is *"Get the right thing done the right way."* I could have told you their mission was something of the sort simply through my personal experience. I am pretty loyal to Les Schwab because they've always shown me they care about providing service the right way and ensure that I don't have any problems when I leave their shop. Their employees exude this mission feeling. If I arrive with a problem, they kick into gear and ensure I leave satisfied. I always feel more like a guest than a customer. They surely coach their employees to do more than expected, because that's been my experience. When I pulled into a Les Schwab store in a small Oregon town with a temporary donut tire on my car after an unfortunate flat tire experience, they fixed my flat for free, and sent me on my way, expressing appreciation for using their tires. If ever I have a question or want reassurance about my tires, they are there. They don't tell me I need brakes if I don't, even after pulling in and telling them I need new brakes. They are willing to check my tires for free and reward me for being a loyal customer. Sometimes the true belief in the mission is tested when a mistake is made. Not all companies are perfect, and this is when the mission comes to life, and you know if the employees believe in it or not.

Years ago, an employee at Les Schwab put the wrong size tires on the front of our car, which then caused the transmission to lock up a few days later. Once brought to their attention by the auto dealership, Les Schwab owned the mistake and replaced the transmission. They handled that situation beyond expectations, and they did "Get the right thing done the right way." If their frontline staff did not know their mission, I don't believe the service they preach would have been delivered in unison with their mission in that situation.

Dutch Bros. Coffee – When I pull up to a Dutch Bros. coffee shop, I am consistently greeted by enthusiastic employees with the music and employees rocking out. They genuinely appear to be enjoying their day and the people they serve. I am always asked about what my day might entail or what's going on in life, and then they listen. I've never once felt like the employees see their work as just a job. They are laughing and having fun together. It's clear all their employees fully understand the brand and mission. Here's what Dutch Bros. has on their website: *"Dutch Bros. wants to empower employees who have shown desire, drive and determination to run a Dutch Bros. location of their own. Growth opportunities are exclusively for existing, qualified Dutch Bros. employees and are closed to the public."* They could not accomplish this if they hired employees who refused to learn the mission of the organization.

Let me share a little of my personal journey working for mission-focused employers that believed their employees needed to believe in the mission as well. After I graduated from college with my business degree in Accountancy, I landed an accounting position at the Girl Scout Council. I had been involved in girl scouting as a child, and knew it could provide a career experience for this new accountant that would be more than simply pushing numbers. Talk about an impactful organization with a compelling mission! The Girl Scouts mission is to *"... build girls of courage, confidence, and character, who make the world a better place."* It may have been easy for me to be distant with their overall mission of building girls to be strong leaders, because after all, how was I going to do that as their "back office" accountant? But I actually found a way to use the mission in my job. I thought of ways that I might provide data analysis to help the organization better understand who they served, and how I could help the troop leaders in providing timely and accurate accounting of troop cookie sale funds by region.

Learning about the tremendous entrepreneurial skills that girls gained through the cookie sales and how they helped build the girls' courage and character, for example, energized me to find ways to use data to show their impact in setting goals to do cool things with their earnings at the troop level. It was equally important for me to understand the various programs and how I might be able to provide insight to the management and board as their staff accountant, in order to serve their mission better. I remember absorbing the mission discussions in many side conversations and staff meetings, and I also participated in volunteer events where girls were present, learning about the impact of the organization on them.

Those activities created an even stronger belief in me around what the organization was all about. So even though I was familiar with this organization before I joined the staff, I still had much to learn and embraced the opportunity to understand the "why" of the organization in every appropriate conversation and meeting. I found ways to provide the board additional reports to help guide the organization. This helped me as discussions with budgeting evolved around the meaningful subsidized programs being delivered, such as camps, and why they were such an integral part of the Girl Scout experience of building courageous girls. Had I focused solely on my accounting responsibilities in that position, and excluded the mission thinking, I could have lost sight of the overall purpose of the organization. It likely would have led to less-than-effective recommendations to the board that may have been contrary to the mission. Knowing the mission created a well-rounded accountant in me for that organization. And let's not forget, it helped me create an elevator speech about the Girl Scouts that I believed in with all my heart, and today I am still an active volunteer for that organization and have motivated dozens of girls and adults to experience what they have to offer.

Today, I am also fortunate to be part of the cooperative mission of "people helping people" in the financial services industry, working for a credit union. When I entered the industry as a Vice President of Finance, my understanding was simply that a credit union was a bank. I began to ask many questions to understand the core mission of credit unions and why they were different. Today, I emphatically support and believe this mission, which goes far beyond managing the flow of our customers' money through everyday checking accounts and auto loans. Our customers are actually members. And we are not a bank. I saw firsthand how we helped member owners get back on their feet after being turned away from other financial institutions.

For example, if we have a member that has made poor decisions with their finances, I saw my credit union truly living the "people helping people" mission. We did not judge, and instead helped get them back on track through smart decisions and a plan. That included a second-chance checking account and participation in our credit builder program. It was more than profitability and risk decisions because we fully lived our mission. Back in 2008 through 2012, we created a second change mortgage program for those great members who lost their homes because of the recession, but needed help to get back into a home and now held jobs. Our mission drove the creation of this program, and it was tremendously successful to both the members and the credit union. No one else that I'm aware of offered what we did. And it was driven by our mission of *"...delivering lifetime personalized banking solutions."* How much more personal can you get than that? Completing the "mission gut check" with various decisions and their relevancy to the mission has kept me grounded for over 20 years with my current employer, and certainly is an important factor as I serve as their President/CEO today. It was important to the board many years ago that I not only had the financial expertise, but that I was also a strong advocate of the industry's mission.

It might go unsaid to some, but employers expect their employees to support the mission in all they do. Looking to promote someone in an organization always includes the consideration as to whether that person has "bought into" the mission. Imagine the confusion if a supervisor leads a group of people and they aren't on board with the mission. It would be like suiting up for a basketball game and wearing a different colored jersey than your teammates. It would be confusing to the coach, the team, and the spectators.

I encourage you to attempt to take this one step further and get the mission of your company ingrained into your heart and soul. Get creative and intentionally study the mission so you can adore it. Get your hands on every mission and/or vision statement your company has created, or anything that remotely looks like it might be one. Different companies call these different things. They may be referred to as value statements, company propositions, a promise to customers, or even a purpose statement. Scour the employee handbook, study the breakroom bulletin board, and digest the company website. Even dig a little deeper and look for tag lines on company stationery, signs, brochures, banners, and even quotes posted in the CEO's office. Ask about the company values and the strategic direction of the organization and how you can contribute towards helping them reach success. Read old employee and customer newsletters and blogs, and talk to the passionate historians in your organization, including long-time employees, vendors, owners, and customers. Be intentional and aware of who in the organization is passionate and embraces the mission. You know, those types that would support the mission through change and challenges.

Stay near to those you can envision supporting with their enthusiasm and belief system, rub shoulders with them, and share thoughts with them to build an even greater buy-in with the purpose. And most importantly, be cautious and never let any particular hypocrite in your organization who doesn't quite live the mission let it impact how you feel about the organization, if one exists. That's their inconsistency to own, not yours.

Once you've scoured the many sources and have done your jewel hunting, begin to look for themes of importance in what the company created for its important mission. What are the common threads you have heard or observed? You should have a good sense by now of who the ideal customer is, what needs you were hired to help with, and how the customer supports the organization's goals. You should also have some knowledge by now on the competitive advantage of what your company offers. Know their mission was likely built over time and created by several leaders in your company, and massaged over many variations of words carefully chosen to focus employees on the most important priority of the company's existence, and how it is communicated to its customers. Don't take lightly what you discover.

Let's talk a little more about the composition of mission statements. Mission statements are typically written and built to support the means for the organization's success. They are carefully crafted words selected to represent something significant, in order to create a focus as employees go about their daily activities in identifying markets, products, services, and competition. Pay close attention to adjectives in mission statements, such as unique, low-cost, or elite. They mean something significant. Some companies might not have their mission statement written down, but the owners or board of directors likely have an idea and passion around what their vision is for the company. Asking them what they have loved about the organization that they might not want to ever change or lose is a good start. If a clearly defined mission doesn't exist or seems stale, go to work on it and create some sample ideas to present to the team or your boss. Be sure to do so with an open mind, as there may be something you have yet to discover about the organization. You will impress them, while building your own passion and understanding of the organization. It will become crystal clear that you have bought into the organization if handled appropriately and with an open mind.

It's important to note that all organizations should have some type of reason for existence, and their differentiation in the competitor space should be identified and be able to be articulated to all the stakeholders of the organization. The type of company does not matter, whether it is a pizza restaurant pushing out thousands of pizzas a year, or the Girl Scouts serving thousands of girls doing great things in the community. All have some purpose and major undertaking driving their existence, and you should be a part of that and know what that unique undertaking is.

So, what if you are the type that just wants to come to work, do your job, and go home? What if you don't care about what the company is trying to accomplish today, but you just want to work and enjoy your job? What if you feel comfortable as long as you are doing what is asked of you right now, and you wish to only worry about that other big picture stuff down the road when someone tells you it is important? Can it be good enough to be a top producer or just show up to work every day with a strong work ethic and do your job, while not sabotaging your career? What employer wouldn't want a bunch of employees who do just that? The answer is those are not bad traits to add to your employment portfolio, and they do contribute to great performance reviews, but consistently possessing those traits and not knowing why it matters for the success of the company will eventually become an obstacle if you want to build your career. And it may actually set you back and cause you to be the least valuable employee on the team if you are in a dynamic, fast-paced, changing organization. I've seen it create employees who become fearful of change, bored, disengaged, and even worse, resentful because others are selected for promotions over them or given new responsibilities. That approach, even when it includes a strong work ethic, may lead to creating a vacuum around you, and eventually cause you to be out of touch. It may even create negativity or skepticism regarding you about the company, because your understanding of the reason behind changes, for the purpose of keeping the mission fresh and relevant, may be misunderstood and take place with a narrow view from you. It's the difference between looking into a mirror versus a kaleidoscope. The risk is in the understanding of any change, or a resistance to it, and becomes more about you in your own understanding rather than clarity around the company's core purpose and direction. So, good work ethic and performance are traits to be commended and often respected, but they generally aren't enough as you climb the ladder or take on more responsibility in order to move up in a company. It is important you don't become stagnant, even if you want to work in your current job forever. You must support the mission and be a cheerleader of it, and everyone around you should know you do!

Along your employment journey, continue to talk to your supervisor one-on-one and with as many executives as you can when the opportunity exists, asking each one to describe what the overall vision is for the company at that time. Dynamic companies change often. Share why you are inquiring, and your desire to be sure you continue to support where the company is going. Be sure to listen carefully in these discussions. Ask questions around the purpose of the organization, the history, and what has made it successful so far. Listen and be alert to capture every detail possible when you see the passion rise to the surface from a leader or leadership team as they talk about their strategic plans, mission, and history. Listen for the "why" that resonates in every new company change that is rolled out. Find a way to embrace that "why" within your own circle of influence in the company. I assure you this information will become invaluable to you later on and keep you grounded when change is par for the course. Keep in mind that as you grow in the organization, you may eventually be that leader who needs to explain all the same information to your employees.

Also understand that a transition will take place as you grow in your career. You will slowly be required to grow from being tactical to being strategic. You will likely be needed to move from being a doer to a little more of a thinker. You will slowly be pulled into conversations about the "why" behind the strategy being discussed in committees or focus groups. Every boss needs critical thinkers on their crew who understand the mission in order for the company to be successful, which is why it is important to master this knowledge. In smaller companies, you might need to be both an executor and a strategic thinker at the same time. No captain wants to be the only one on his ship that holds the navigation course knowledge, and leaders gravitate towards employees who share their sights on the future.

Let me give you another example of why knowing and supporting the mission is important. I recently held a focus group session of customers and asked them what they wished my company provided for them in order for them to continue to be in love with us. The expansion of our normal hours to include Saturday hours was mentioned a few times. This was great feedback because we had already determined we would be adding Saturday hours to fulfill our mission and serve our customers more effectively. Our supporters, namely our customers who were already opening up their wallets for our employees to earn a paycheck, were telling us what they wanted as their vision for our company, and we had the option to listen or not.

Part of our mission statement at the credit union states, *"provide a financial experience with a unique style."* So, if we stayed true to our current Monday through Friday hourly structure, knowing Saturdays are a preferred day for many people that may have that specific day off work, I would say we would not be fulfilling our mission of being unique, and the experience is not one to brag about in our customers' eyes. We included the word "unique" in our mission statement for a reason, so it is important to ensure we were fulfilling our promise. Unique would be providing them an opportunity to do their banking outside of the dreaded high-traffic times to and from work. Understanding this then becomes easier for me as an employee to understand the "why" behind this decision and support it. It's easier because it's no longer all about the change for me having to work Saturdays now.

By understanding the "why" in this case, I can now claim the mission as being part of something greater. The employees will embrace this change positively because they know how the customers will benefit, and they'll likely support the leadership team's decision and rise above any challenges as a result. Employees who choose to focus on the negative effect of this change on them personally, for example, likely will have no better solution to serving our member's needs on Saturdays and may come across as not supporting the mission. They may even misstep if they never invested the time to learn the why behind it. Never discount the power of being noticed as the employee who supports a difficult decision, or the negative power of being branded as the employee who is selfishly resistant to difficult changes. Leaders notice, and they discuss these observations months later when the next career advancement discussion is happening to move the organization forward.

Imagine being the boss's right hand when your company explains a recent change or new direction to its employees. If that announcement doesn't include the mission or vision, and how the change will support building on that mission, there is risk that the intentions surrounding the change will simply be misunderstood, and its deployment will stumble. If the company has a team of visionless executors at the top, and the long list of projects executed by doers lacking an understanding of how it all contributes to a central mission, for example, it will feel like a bunch of finches on steroids. These finches will likely flutter about and work hard to build their nests under many eaves, fighting for power in certain places but not really understanding why.

If this is you, you may be setting yourself up for failure, and also slip into a tendency to feel negative towards the leadership in your organization, which almost always becomes a career killer. The most important way to get recognized as an exceptional employee worthy of advancement is to already be known as the employee who "gets it" and supports it. Opportunities are likely to be presented to the employee who understands what success looks like with each initiative or project, and how it will be completed to support the strategic plan and budget. Be the employee who continuously knows and ensures you are supporting the intended direction of the leadership of the company.

Think about this question for a moment: What boss wants to hire someone to drive their team's success when they know that the employee is coming on board with a mismatch in beliefs about the direction? Most smart and strategic leaders won't take that risk, even if that candidate's technical skills are solid. Playing tug-of-war with employees around the mission of your organization is no fun for leaders. It would be like hiring an employee from a competitor that has a less desirable product, and then letting them bring that product into your company, knowing it doesn't support the current mission or your high-quality standards. Synergy is powerful in building something great, and it is created when everyone is producing and improving the same product or service with a common vision, and not fighting road blocks along the way. Balking at the mission is simply a distraction and is a trait that most bosses will avoid in their selection of moving people into new opportunities.

So what if you have invested in your understanding of the mission of the company and you have some ideas to support something new? Let me be very clear that this chapter's message does not mean you must agree with every part of the strategic positioning of the company. In fact, each employee has something to offer that someone on the leadership team likely has not thought of or does not yet hold close to their chest. There is value in learning many perspectives and insights. However, be very careful how new ideas that don't support the vision are delivered, and more importantly, how stubborn you might become if they are not received well. As a leader in my company, I appreciate hearing new ways of thinking, and often ask employees their input through focus groups, coaching sessions, project teams, and surveys. I do my best to stay welcoming in my demeanor to solicit ideas from every employee. It is something I work on every day.

Questions must be welcomed, as long as they are delivered professionally. Be careful they are not presented in a manipulative manner, as that breaks down trust of motivation on a broader scale that is difficult to overcome. I know my employees are typically more in tune to the customers of our organization than I am, simply because they see or talk to them every day. In fact, a few years ago, I had my team at various levels in the organization track the number of times they interacted with our customers (in our case, our member owners). The following chart reflects how often each of the different levels within our organization connected to one of our member owners in a month. This data confirmed the criticalness that we as leaders listen carefully to our frontline team, and all the way up the organization chart, to welcome their input regarding what our customers want.

Member Interactions per Month

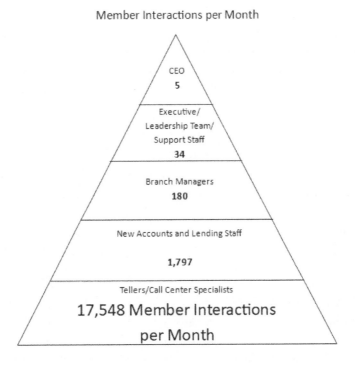

CEO
5

Executive/
Leadership Team/
Support Staff
34

Branch Managers
180

New Accounts and Lending Staff

1,797

Tellers/Call Center Specialists
17,548 Member Interactions
per Month

Therefore, it's very important to me that I hear what my team is hearing and the brilliant ideas they might have to serve our customers better or make their work as employees more efficient. Their connection to the primary customers is so strong that their input may actually drive a change to a company's mission statement if they were to hear a resounding need for a different direction, for example. But be careful here. Unfortunately, I also see many employees sabotage their careers because they form strong opinions or a dislike with new initiatives, and then buckle in to take the leadership team on a closed-minded ride in the process. If you want to take your boss for a ride, take them on a ride through the world of wonder and insight, a positive ride of educating and seeking to understand, and avoid the dangerous ride where you dig in your heels and cause your brakes to lock up and skid over the cliff. Know that although your boss wants your insight, they may not need your vote. You need to find a way to support their direction without resistance.

Even more importantly than bringing an idea to your boss is bringing an idea that comes with a better solution, especially when the idea is addressing a challenge or problem. In addition, you must include how it supports the mission, strategic plan, and budget. It's not good enough to simply push for an idea that will drive more sales or more net income if your ideas are contrary to the mission. Sales managers should avoid focusing solely on the gross sales goals, for example, and instead look at the whole picture of profitability and the impact on the customers' long-term satisfaction about the product or service. You should complete an honest mission and culture check before you even present your idea. It will allow you to identify your intended goals, personal biases, and even potential implications if your idea goes poorly. So, as you see, everything is more successful if you invest in understanding the purpose of the company and how your input will be supporting it today and long term.

As I mentioned earlier, I've been blessed to have worked for organizations with strong missions most of my career. They have been more focused on the mission of whom they serve than the outcomes they generate, although they never lost sight of the outcomes. Growth and profitability have always been important, even in my strong mission-oriented non-profit organizations. Being prosperous is one thing; being prosperously profitable is even better. In my current role as President/CEO of Icon Credit Union, our mission includes building financial success for our members. Our members are our customers. Therefore, it is more important for me to monitor how we are improving our members' financial lives than simply monitoring growth and profitability.

That being said, I strongly support the need for a budget that provides net income to continue providing new services to our members to build their financial success, and also ensure we are here tomorrow for them. It's more important that I can share how our members might save an average of more than $2,000 on every auto loan by financing with us than how many auto loans the team closed yesterday. It's important to know that my team is mentoring our customers by helping them create budgets, compared to simply opening up as many checking accounts as possible and then sending them on their way. The question I have asked is if my member service folks don't believe in our mission, how will they be able to show that same passion on the front line when working with members who need financial help? The answer is maybe they can, but I know this would be to a much smaller degree.

This is where building a strong culture to support your mission comes in once again. I do support that if you invest in your internal culture, followed by investing in your customer delivery and experience, the financial success will come to reinvest back into your customers' needs and wants, and your employees as well. It's a great circle of life in any organization. None of the three components (internal culture, customer experience, financial outcome) work in isolation from each other. In my current organization, we invested heavily in creating cultural and perception values several years ago, and today we are rated high in many peer categories, including being rated in the top 2% of the healthiest credit unions in the country, and we are named one of the *Best Places to Work in Idaho*. All three pieces work together for us, starting with a compelling mission and clarity with our purpose. These definitions provide a different perspective of leadership focus—I learned them many years ago from Michael Neill, President of ServiStar Consulting, LLC.

Outcome-Based Leadership
The leader has a primary focus on the **desired outcomes**, and leads to develop an organization that will *produce those outcomes.*
vs.
Missional-Based Leadership
The leader has a primary focus on the **purpose of the organization, relative to those it serves**, and leads to develop an organization that will *fulfill that purpose.*

I propose that companies can become successful with either of these types of different leadership focus areas, but *awesomeness* comes from Missional-Based organizations. It's too easy to slip into undesirable behavior and pressure if you are solely concerned about outcomes at any cost, regardless of the mission and culture. And remember, it would be very difficult to be awesome if your entire team wasn't fully invested in your cultural values and mission.

Finally, know that although it's the senior team level that created the mission and purpose, it's *yours* to understand, support, embrace, provide input on, and positively contribute to for every minute you are on the payroll. Being at odds with the mission and staying that way will send a message that you choose to have a ball and chain around your waist and want to stay stuck in your career. Avoid becoming emotionally disenchanted with this role in the company if it isn't your job to own. Don't take differences of opinions personally, but instead advocate for the purpose your leadership is building and focus on how you can help.

Know there are always exceptions to every rule. For example, I'm not going to support any mission that isn't full of integrity and ethical in nature. However, I do believe every employee has the obligation to take situations to the leadership that are considered contrary to the mission. I instruct my employees that they need to work within the chain of command and the organizational structure for consistent communication, respect, and building accountability. But if ever there is a time when they observe something that is illegal, unethical, or immoral, they should feel comfortable going to any leader in the company and reporting it without retaliation. If you are ever in this situation, it's important to state whether your observations are fact based or simply a suspicion. Never risk your personal brand, character, or moral standards for a company that exhibits practices that are contrary to your standards. That being said, be sure you are basing your assessment on truth and not emotional discontent or gossip, or you may assess a situation incorrectly. It's also important you don't spread the bad news you have discovered to those who have no reason to know. That only hurts the company and can make the situation far worse.

In summary, if you wish to build your career, it's a requirement that you live and breathe the mission of your company. Don't sabotage your career by opposing any decision by the leadership in your organizations. First, seek to understand the mission. Then, learn about the purpose leading up to the decision or change and how it will support the success of the organization. Never forget to seek to understand first before you propose different insights, and if needed, oppose only long enough to share your opinion, ask for consideration, and then step back and support the leader's final decision or preference. When you share your opinion, be sure to include your suggested solution if you are addressing a recommendation or discussing a problem. You will instantly be seen as a team player, supportive of the company's goals, and most importantly, there to serve the very customers who provide the funds that land in your paycheck.

8: Step Up and Serve on Boards and Committees

Serve and learn. Volunteering to serve on boards and committees will pay back tenfold. How much are you willing to volunteer to serve on other committees and boards, both internally and externally? The assessment below provides some questions for you to consider in assessing your willingness to expand your skills and increase your exposure in this area.

Quick Sabotage Assessment: Do I volunteer and serve to expand my horizons and increase my exposure to different skills, people, and situations?

CAREER BUILDING CHARACTERISTICS	Y/N	CAREER SABOTAGING CHARACTERISTICS	Y/N
Do I submit my name when the company is looking for Christmas Committee or summer picnic volunteers?		Do I stay quiet because I don't like to plan parties?	
Do I offer to help with the company group planning to participate in the Paint the Town Day?		Do I stay quiet because I don't really want to spend my Saturday painting?	
Do I seek out opportunities to serve on other boards or committees for local non-profits?		Do I keep my volunteer efforts slim because I'm not sure I want to commit to other activities? Do I avoid volunteering because I don't really know the individuals who I will be serving with?	

(Quick Sabotage Assessment, Cont.)

CAREER BUILDING CHARACTERISTICS	Y/N	CAREER SABOTAGING CHARACTERISTICS	Y/N
Do I look for opportunities to bring into my workplace to solicit volunteers that can bring positive exposure to my company?		*Do I dislike that my company is involved in the community, or am I okay as long as they don't ask me to volunteer?*	
If I am a supervisor, am I a good role model with volunteerism, even if socializing and volunteering are not my thing?		*If I am a supervisor, do I simply make it clear I don't like this stuff and refuse to participate unless I am forced or begged to do so?*	

Volunteering to serve is critical in building your career opportunities. The type of people that raise their hand and volunteer to serve are typically incredible and courageous leaders. Surround yourself with these people. When you bring a group of people together that hold a kindred spirit of volunteerism to work together for a great purpose, magic happens. You meet incredible people, learn how to communicate to reach a common goal, and build a healthy network of professionals around you. Some of my wisest, most courageous, and healthiest friends in my professional world are those I've met through serving on boards and committees. I am a volunteer at heart because I believe it fills your soul. Not everyone is as committed to volunteerism as I am, and they don't have to be. But knowing the benefits of this, even if you are not a natural in serving, is important.

Volunteering for those causes that serve the underserved or less fortunate keeps life in perspective for me. When you volunteer at a Special Olympics event, for example, your perspective from that moment onward changes. When you see a troubled teen get the help they need and eventually go on to college, it fills your soul. If you aren't currently serving, think about a non-profit that serves an audience you are passionate about helping, and call them today to get on a committee or find some way to get in the door to help them at an upcoming event.

In my career, I have volunteered and served on numerous boards and committees, many working boards and some advisory-only. I've served alongside some of the most intelligent and wise professionals I've ever met in my career. My service work has forced me to become exposed to issues, projects, and courageous conversations I would never have been exposed to if I didn't say "yes" when asked. And many I simply sought out because I had a passion to help in certain areas that were needed. I recall many board conversations where challenging my strategic mind was required, and speaking truth into conversations as an outside person was needed. I've learned how to manage volunteers and be an effective volunteer.

Volunteering for local non-profit organizations is only one great way to learn and gain skills that can help your career. Volunteering to serve on committees and focus groups in your own company is another great way. The leadership of your organization knows who is willing to give and serve on company event committees, for example, such as the Christmas Committee, retreats, and the annual company summer picnic. Many organizations also form focus groups for a specific company initiative, and often the employees who are asked to serve on these interesting focus groups are those the leadership see step up on other committees. By joining the company groups mentioned, you will have a greater opportunity to rub shoulders with the leadership in your company, different employees from other departments, and many times, influential community leaders. Your network will open up beyond your own circle and create a new invaluable circle of influence. It takes a commitment on your part, but a worthy one.

I do recommend before you ever step onto a board or committee, that you understand what is going to be asked of you in time, talent, and treasure. You will want to know what they may expect from your organization and your time during the workday, and ensure your organization is willing and has the sufficient resources to support it. If it isn't a good fit, keep looking to find an opportunity that is. Also, be sure the cause or core mission is one that supports your personal belief system, as well as being something your company would be proud to support. You want to avoid a conflict in this area if possible. It may be dangerous for your company to support a cause or organization that is controversial or political in nature, so a good dialogue before you commit is important.

It is always crucial to be sure that your volunteer service level improves your brand and does not create a negative impact on it. I shared a little about this in the chapter on creating your personal brand. If you commit, fully commit. You are a representative of your own self, and also your company. You don't want to be known as that person from Company X that never shows up to meetings, shows up late or unprepared, or is obnoxiously aggressive in your volunteer communication or participation. Never lose sight that you are representing your company as well as yourself in your volunteer activities.

Also, remember you should not feel like you have to take over the non-profit or become operationally involved when that is not your role. Most non-profits have paid staff to run the daily operations of the organization, and your job as a volunteer is to support their efforts that they deem most helpful. That doesn't mean you shouldn't bring new strategic ideas and thinking to the table, but be careful that you are not aggressive in trying to take over. And always keep your personal agenda in check, as it can be contrary to the good of the order of where you are serving. You will gain respect if you can find a way to balance this. If you are overly critical of the President of your Home Owner's Association (HOA) and communicate unprofessionally at your HOA meetings, for example, it can cause you and your career more damage than if you didn't serve at all. If you want to gain a tremendous opportunity to improve your communication skills and professional reputation, join your HOA and make it your personal mission to change the professional environment of that association!

The same is true of Parent Teacher Associations (PTAs). Both opportunities attract participants with heavy personal agendas and they typically need strong unemotional leaders to chart the way, and are much more effective if this can be achieved. Volunteering on the fund development committees of non-profit organizations will significantly build your relationship and communication skills, not to mention project management skills if you are tasked with planning a fundraising event. And you will have the opportunity to connect with some key players in your community in the process. Volunteering to serve on a search committee for a new Executive Director will provide you some great recruitment skills. Serving on a strategic planning committee will give you some great strategic thinking and goal-setting skills. As you can see, many opportunities will come your way if you step up and serve. Also, never be afraid to step up and serve on a small committee before you get asked to serve on a more powerful group, such as the board of directors. Many large non-profits wish to try you out first to see how you communicate and support the organization and to test your commitment level. It's always a perfect first step to join a committee before taking the leap and serving at a higher level on a board.

You might work for a smaller company that does not have official committees or boards, but the concept still applies—when you see an opportunity to help others, jump in!

And let's not forget the opportunity to build your resume in the process of volunteering and serving. Employers often look to your resume to see what your community affiliations are. It simply shows good leadership experience and intent. Be cautious of having your only volunteer activities lie with your church or children's school. It's better than no volunteer work and certainly every church and school needs member and parent participation, but it can have less of an impact than if you step onto another broader board or committee. I recommend both!

9: Use the Power of One Voice

In Chapter Six, I shared much insight about the importance of supporting your boss. Much time was spent in Chapter Seven discussing the importance of supporting the mission of the organization. Equally important is finding your voice that is consistent with the leadership's voice of your company, in order to support strategies and changes consistently. I will speak to this in greater detail later in this chapter, but the single most important takeaway here is understanding the critical role that an aligned voice plays in building trust, creating engaged employees, and perfecting your brand. This chapter extends the goal of a unified voice with your boss to benefit the mission of the whole company. This is the stage where your professional approach to work and life begins to put you at an executive level of thinking and leadership.

When you are able to become "one," you are much more effective delivering any message within the company, both internally and externally. You must be able to articulate the reason for a change and support it in unison with the management's intentions. Most organizations must experience many changes or they will die, so get used to doing this and how to communicate effectively, especially when you have less-than-desirable news to deliver or support. Master the skill of supporting the latest focus or change and delivering the message to your peers and employees on your team with one positive, unified voice. That one voice should be in alignment with the company's voice, the department next door, and the messaging to your customers.

The following are questions you can ask yourself to assess your own ability to lead with one voice and support the direction of the organization with the same. I'll go into each of these in greater detail in this chapter. How well do you rate yourself in your ability to speak with one voice within your organization, and are you supporting the mission or sabotaging it?

Quick Sabotage Assessment: Do I consistently support the company with "one voice"? Do others believe I believe in the company?

CAREER BUILDING CHARACTERISTICS	Y/N	CAREER SABOTAGING CHARACTERISTICS	Y/N
Do I support the culture of the "CEO at every desk" mentality, meaning, do I make decisions in alignment with what the CEO would make that support building a successful company? Do others see me as a person that believes in the direction my CEO or supervisor is striving to lead, and do my actions support that direction, even when faced with resistance by others? Do I consistently reflect that "I agree and support the direction?"		Do I put the burden of the culture on the CEO and make comments or act in ways that are contrary to what the CEO is attempting to accomplish for the company? Do I ever infer that the CEO is the "bad guy?" If the CEO or superiors were part of my discussions with team members, would they feel or sense my lack of support and synergy for the direction?	
Do I step up and address inconsistencies that come to my attention professionally?		Do I show favoritism depending on the person, or department, because it is just easier than facing resistance?	
Do I present tough news and own the explanation and reasons for it, such as unfortunate, impending staffing cuts? Am I well prepared with how to explain the release of bad news?		Do I discuss how it is and then communicate poorly that it wasn't my decision?	

(Quick Sabotage Assessment, Cont.)

CAREER BUILDING CHARACTERISTICS	Y/N	CAREER SABOTAGING CHARACTERISTICS	Y/N
Do I share the responsibility and carry the message of the importance of adhering to my company's policies and procedures as if they were my own, because they are "our" procedures and policies to own?		*Do I selectively decide which procedures or policies I will follow, and find ways to sabotage certain ones? Do I insinuate, even with just body language, that I am not in support of the current procedures and policies created by the CEO or my superiors? Do I ever send a message that a procedure is stupid or wastes time? Do I share that I don't support the existing policies to my peers or direct reports?*	
Do I ensure that all of my executive team members are on the same page with the reasons for the change before I communicate it?		*Do I roll things out carelessly because the timing worked for me, then deal with the questions because I wasn't prepared for ensuring all departments were ready?*	
Do I deliver a new strategic direction to my team as "my" or "our" direction, and with excitement, even if I disagree or know it may not be received well?		*Do I present the ideas as coming from my CEO because it is easier for me, and my team won't feel negative thoughts towards me personally if they disagree? Would I rather say, "management said," rather than say, "I believe?"*	

(Quick Sabotage Assessment, Cont.)

CAREER BUILDING CHARACTERISTICS	Y/N	CAREER SABOTAGING CHARACTERISTICS	Y/N
Do I encourage my department to be consistent with following the personnel policies so we have company-wide adoption and consistency? Am I a good role model?		*Do I allow my department to do things a little differently than other departments are expected to do because it is easier than to boldly and courageously address situations to gain consistency company-wide? Do I act inconsistently because I can get away with it or for my personal benefit?*	
Do I expect management to follow the same general guidelines and cultural values as non-management employees?		*Do I use my authority to ask for exceptions not offered to others? Do I abuse my rank or position and portray an executive privilege attitude?*	
Do I show courage when my peers or employees ask for exceptions that are knowingly against the company direction or policy, and do I take the time to explain why they were put in place or how they protect the company and support consistency?		*Do I go ahead and honor the exception and just address it later if it becomes known or causes any problems? Do I ever say, "Just don't tell anyone I approved this?"*	
Do I work directly with my employees on areas for improvement and challenges that are brought to my attention from a different department, and communicate as if the issue is coming from me, as their direct supervisor?		*Do I blame another department's employee for the discovery of the problem or violation and refer to them as the source when the problem was identified?*	
Do I support the organization and the direction publicly outside the company?		*Do I negatively discuss my indifference to the direction and concern for management's decisions?*	

In this chapter, much of the discussion is focused on how you support and deliver a message in your organization. Maybe it is how you share a new direction or bad news. As a result, I'm going to speak mostly to leaders in the organization, although supporting the organization with a consistent message is important at all levels and to any career. This gets more important as you climb the ladder or earn more responsibility of communicating messages. Being a leader in any organization takes strong communication skills and a whole lot of courage. If you are a person who avoids discussions that might not be received well and latch onto comfort and harmony over discomfort that might take place in a needed crucial conversation, this chapter is for you. Also, if you want to be the hero often and not rock the boat with your peers or team when coaching or when new messages need to be delivered, stay with me in this chapter. Courage is needed in order to own the direction of the company and carry it on your shoulders as the leader, and it has many benefits in keeping the culture strong and being supportive of management. Your career will become stale or include distrust if you can't master the skill of speaking as one voice, and that voice is the company's desired voice.

So what does the term "one voice" mean? One voice means communicating in a way that matches the company's desired message when relaying any type of decision, change, or disciplinary action. You communicate with full conviction that you believe in the message you are stating, even if you disagree ever so slightly. One voice means you should never fall into a weak state of referring to a decision made by the CEO, or another manager, as not yours or one you don't wholeheartedly support. Making a statement such as, "Carol wants us to start doing XYZ," is simply inappropriate if you insinuate in any way that you don't support it equally. In fact, it's even risky, and there is really no reason to even bring in Carol's name, but instead bring forth the topic as your idea or recommendation. It's important to deliver the strategic direction and important decisions as your voice, one unified company voice with the company and all of management, and one you believe in and support.

I can't stress this enough! Simply put, if you want to work in a great culture and grow your career, don't blame your boss for things. Never represent the initiative or change as you simply being the messenger of the initiative, especially if you are in leadership. It may be easier in the moment, but you will build a team that doesn't trust you or management, causing disengaged and confused employees at times. They'll wonder where you stand and what you are protecting them from.

Distrust can become rampant if this is mishandled because, after all, who can they trust when they get conflicting opinions as to where a decision was born or supported by? If you misstep and lean on Carol as the sole creator or owner of the decision, it will leave a doubt in your audience's mind as to whether you or certain management team members support it, and if the employees should even trust Carol's expertise and decision-making skills if they disagree with the decision. They'll be left to wonder if the message is yours or the boss's, and who is not being upfront. You also put Carol in a very bad position, as your employees will now wonder if the leader, Carol, has what it takes to make the appropriate decisions they disagree with. This is because you just planted the seed that maybe Carol isn't as intelligent as she needs to be, but you send the message you are. It's self-centered and shows a weakness on your part if you undermine Carol. Phrases such as, "I'm just the messenger," are completely inappropriate. Leaders must share and own the direction within the company. It's simply better to rephrase the message to be something like, "We've been working on a solution for XYZ, and I believe it will be a great change." It is extremely harmful to an organization if you skirt around owning the message, typically because you personally lack the courage or communication skills, and it will become a serious obstacle in your career. You may feel like your employees support you and you become the hero in the moment, but they will soon become disgruntled with the organization as a whole, and see you going down a different track than the CEO. That track is a dangerous one in your career. Eventually, your employees will become disillusioned with the company's overall leadership and leave, which is something that will eventually hurt you as a leader.

If you struggle with speaking in one voice, it is important to ask yourself why, and understand that it may be because you have a difficult time delivering crucial conversations or news that is not rosy and positive. Or maybe you become defensive when challenged by an aspect of the decision and you don't know how to respond quickly. Maybe you simply want to be liked and be the hero, but these weaknesses and faults as a leader will turn deadly when your team eventually sees you as a coward or a leader with double standards. Employees see right through this when it happens. Never kid yourself into thinking that they don't see it or that it is better for them.

Let me give you an example to illustrate the "one voice" concept. Let's imagine that the entire leadership team, including a vice president named James, has decided to increase the pricing of a particular product line, knowing the sales staff will be disappointed because it may affect their sales short-term and their individual commissions. When James shares this decision directly with his team, he makes a mistake and shares it as a decision made by the CEO, and that he wasn't part of the process. He doesn't use the words "we" in his delivery, and immediately his entire team is disgruntled and upset with the CEO, and eventually it impacts how they feel about the entire organization. And they may even wonder about James, who didn't stand up against the decision when it came to be for his team? It now becomes personal against the CEO, and even more so than their dislike for the change itself.

First and foremost, James's actions did not protect the CEO or senior management team by his delivery message choice, and it put the CEO and the company in harm's way. Second, James didn't own any part of this decision from the leadership team that he himself is a part of, and therefore, will have a difficult time working his team through it and gaining buy-in if they have issues with it. Teams sometimes see through this and sometimes not. There will always be a shadow of doubt cast on the shoulders of any leadership team member named as the scapegoat, in this case the CEO. This has the potential to create an ugly divide in the company, and if you are in leadership, it can be dangerous to the company and your career. James's team, in this case, will become disgruntled, and they will continue to build resentment because they'll likely never have the opportunity to fully discuss with the CEO the reason for the change. James thinks he is okay because he didn't have to be the owner, but in building his career, he makes a fatal mistake, as the CEO will eventually feel the discontent by a lack of support and understanding from his team. In addition, James will likely have higher turnover in his department, hurting his long-term growth, because who wants to work for a company where the leadership is not in sync and they have a cowardly boss?

So what should have happened? James should have positively relayed the researched and well-thought-out decision by the entire leadership team and why the change supports the company's mission. He then should have explained the change in detail, while supporting the team through what the change means to them and why it was made for the organization. Ongoing conversations will then be held as the change is implemented, and James would own the various challenges and work through them with his team directly, earning him respect. His enthusiasm for the change will build enthusiasm in others. His support for the decision will build support. No other leader should own this decision except James when he presents it. All leaders must support it equally with their own teams. Using phrases such as, "the entire leadership team" is much more effective. This way, his team can ask him questions and he can provide the hands-on explanations, talk through the challenges, encourage his team through it, and speak on his own behalf and his team's behalf.

I've seen this simple communication mishap destroy how people feel about the leader, and yet the direct supervisor thinks they escaped the difficult situation by being nice, weak, and cowardly, which shifts the responsibility of the decision to the CEO. The culture pays deeply in this situation. Imagine the next great decision to be communicated and if his team will trust the explanation provided by James for it. Will they be skeptical? The answer is likely yes, creating a challenge for James, even though he might feel he skated by an uncomfortable experience with this one. Oftentimes, it will even lead to employees going to other leaders to get the inside scoop, because James has created an environment of distrust.

The same is true when one leader identifies an area that needs to be brought to the attention of another department lead. In this case, the department lead should meet with the employee who needs coached, for example, and must own the delivery of the coaching opportunity and not pull in the other leader's name who observed the coaching opportunity and expressed the original concern. If you see an employee that is not yours do something against policy, bring it to their supervisor's attention quickly. Let's just say that Sandy is observed as consistently arriving to work late by Paul. Paul then brings this to the attention of Sandy's supervisor. What is critical is when Sandy's supervisor addresses the problem with Sandy, they should own this as their coaching to work through with Sandy. Sandy's supervisor is the person accountable to Sandy and responsible for growing Sandy and holding her accountable. She should not even mention Paul's name, as that is unimportant. She can simply say that it has been observed, but even then, only if it is needed.

Too often, the supervisor receiving the complaint will mention who noticed the area of needed improvement, rather than simply working through the issue directly with their team member. It's not important who saw the area of concern or training opportunity. What's more important is that the employee is coached on how to prevent it in the future. What happens when a supervisor shares with their employee that another department lead saw them violating a policy, for example? Immediately, that employee asks themselves, "Why didn't they feel comfortable bringing the issue to my attention directly?" It becomes personal. "Why did they feel the need to take it to my supervisor? Why did they get me in trouble?" All these questions are then followed by the fearful thoughts of, "I wonder how the other department lead now feels about me? Do I need to go to them and also explain what happened, or will my boss do that fairly for me? Will I now be judged by two members of leadership instead of one?" These are valid questions from an employee's perspective. The reason the direct supervisor needs to be brought in the know is simply the benefit of following the chain of command, because it is important the direct supervisor knows where their employees need coaching and training, since they are ultimately the one responsible for their team's performance. As you can see, a simple communication mishap as mentioned above will cause the employee to immediately begin to build resentment, distrust, and a questionable fear around it all. Coaching and mentoring doesn't have to become personal, but it often does if the direct supervisor handles it poorly.

Many organizations hold meetings with staff where they discuss opportunities and challenges with them, even though the employees may not be their direct reports. The "one voice" is still equally important in these meetings. Avoid putting your boss in precarious situations by going over his head with your ideas or complaints, especially if you have not previously discussed with him or her directly. If his boss is smart and a good leader, he'll pull you and your boss into a discussion anyway, so go about discussing your thoughts with your boss first to gain a resolution.

There are, of course, exceptions to every best practice while building your career, and this area is no exception. An exception might include an observation about immoral or unethical behavior that may be best handled directly with the human resources department or going above your boss's head. Be careful, though, that you remain unemotional, use facts to support your complaint, and be clear to avoid making a false accusation. Accusing someone of something simply because you want to get them in trouble or dislike them can be seriously detrimental to your career, so be sure you are acting in good faith and with the facts. Too often, the fear of retaliation sets in and the right people who will listen and address needed concerns are not informed. This is why it is important you build honest, quality relationships with the leaders in your company. Notice, I did not say fake or brown-nosed relationships. These are often seen through as a mask, which can hurt the trust from your leadership. Earn by doing, not by being a smooth talker. If you have true knowledge of corruption with the owner or senior leadership, for example, your only choice may be to change employers, but do your best to communicate with documented facts should you be unfortunate enough to be in this situation.

The worst path of action you can take is show up at an exit interview and unload, firing a list of bullets. You will likely lose credibility if you have not attempted to have a fact-filled professional discussion and give the organization an opportunity to improve. Be careful not to hide behind an ugly letter you send on your way out either. Firing an ugly letter off to the CEO or owner, or the board of directors, without the effort to simply have a discussion, is cowardly and ineffective. It's passive aggressive behavior and the only one that loses in these cases is typically the sender. Yes, you might feel like you are exposing an uncomfortable situation, but without the willingness to have a discussion to seek information, there's little value and these letters typically just get filed. A better approach is to schedule a meeting with the leadership and include the person you have issue with, as hearing all perspectives is important. The respect you will gain by handling yourself professionally on the way out of an organization is just as important as when you joined the organization and were an employee, even if it's going to be very uncomfortable.

In my organization, we use a great tool of holding one-up coaching sessions. One-up sessions are conducted semi-annually, where each leader meets with their direct report's employees. These sessions can be an opportunity to hear about any major unethical, immoral, or illegal activity if the right questions are asked, such as "Are you aware of any activity or employee in our organization who may not be upholding our high standards of integrity and ethics?" I have found these sessions to be a tremendous opportunity to learn more about the support of your culture values and your customers' needs from their perspective, and less about tattling. Be careful if you hold these sessions, though, because it is critical all supervisors be carefully trained to avoid any missteps if an employee uses them as a gripe session or jumping the chain of command. You want one-up sessions to be constructive and supporting the one voice practice. I have utilized a series of questions scripted in advance. Here are some of them.

- What is going well in your career at Company XYZ?
- Where do you need additional resources to succeed, if any?
- What products or services are our customers asking for that we don't offer today?
- Is there anywhere in the company where you have observed we are not living our cultural values?

One-up coaching sessions are also great opportunities to hear what the company should continue doing more of and what they might consider to stop doing. If the employees are closer to the customers you serve than you are, you can learn much about their wants and competition. The sessions can also provide opportunities to connect with employees. They can provide some great insight into how you might better support their leaders (your direct reports) in mentoring them. I value these meetings, but have learned it requires a conscious effort to pay close attention to how I respond when concerns or complaints are shared. They can be ripe for strategically placed complaints about the employee's supervisor. If the conversation goes in that dangerous direction, make it clear that you are willing to listen, as long as they are willing to be in the next conversation as needed, but you may help brainstorm a resolution that will work to improve the organization that they can own and take action on. I remind employees often that we are an organization of open communication and will work together for solutions. One-up conversations of any kind can always improve relationships across all sectors in the organization if handled well and contain the important one voice concept.

Finally, for CEOs, be cautious about communicating direction from the board or owners of your company if they are not employees, blaming the board of directors or owners of the company in a particular direction you may not support. It is just as important—even if you are the CEO—that you own it yourself and deliver the direction as one voice here too. It can be tempting to fall into this trap innocently, and use the "board's direction" as your communication of a strategy you might disagree with, rather than simply owning it as one vision. It's completely acceptable to communicate and mention your board as having a shared vision and strategic direction, but be careful with those disjointed or confusing strategies. It can have the inherent risk and the same challenges discussed above if you don't speak as one voice, even at the board level, because now it becomes more about a potential concern around the board's knowledge and expertise, rather than your own leadership and trust that everyone is moving down the same track. If you are the CEO, own the board's and owner's direction as your vision: one vision.

In summary, always communicate the company's direction to your team as a representative of an entire leadership team that owns the direction. Slow down your communication to make sure all departments and leaders are on the same page and communicating consistently. Take the time to create talking points around every significant change that everyone buys into and make them accessible to the entire team to ensure more consistent messaging occurs at all levels. Roleplay the messaging together as a leadership team because this is where the weaknesses will show up, and you can reinforce your expectations of the messaging and provide any additional training if needed. This is critical and avoids many mishaps with how employees may feel about a particular change and the organization.

If you are a cowardly leader in your organization that is fearful of delivering tough news, you will likely be an ineffective leader long term and be passed over for promotions. You will create distrust with the rest of your team and even though you gain a "hero" status in the short term, your team members will eventually want some bench strength and revolt against you. In addition, you will create a great divide and distrust among your peers and the CEO, as they will be unsure if you will be blaming them for all the difficult news and will not appreciate having the target on their back. Finally, it is a good reminder that "one voice" refers to all employees supporting the mission, not just leadership, in your organization.

10: Minimize Socializing with Employees Outside of Work

Great cultures promote employees working hard and playing hard together. It's important that employees build enjoyable relationships with those they often spend half of their waking hours with. In this chapter, I will share some recommendations on how to appropriately fraternize with your coworkers and employees outside of your normal working hours, and how to do so without causing challenges in the workplace and sabotaging your career. Socializing with coworkers outside of work deserves special and calculated attention.

Know that it isn't typically appropriate for an employer to control what their coworkers and employees do on their personal time outside of work. If they choose to join forces and fraternize with others after hours, they typically have that choice. So in this chapter, similar to many chapters in this book, I will share my opinion about honoring best practices and not putting yourself in a situation where a perceived misconduct or risky behavior might take place, causing others to assume unprofessional behavior on your part, and thereby hurting your brand and career. Sometimes, we simply have to choose to avoid situations that may lead to a perceived negative effect on ourselves as professionals. It's not worth the risk to participate in certain activities. As you know by now after reading the prior chapters, most of this book is about identifying those things that could "potentially" put you at risk of sabotaging your career, even if you have good intentions around them in the moment.

Know that fraternizing through activities with coworkers off the clock can lead to undesirable perceptions, misinterpreted relationships, incorrect intentions and judgment, harmful gossip, jealousy, and many more negative consequences. Although there are some positive effects, such as stronger friendships, understanding each other at a deeper level, and learning about each other's strengths, the positive effects oftentimes are overshadowed by a whole quandary of negative consequences for you and your team. This is true more often in smaller companies and in those situations where you find employees who work in the same division or department, and that of a smaller team or group. But being cautious in large organizations is a sound practice as well.

Potential risk is always a concern in a supervisor and subordinate relationship with any fraternizing on a mere social level with no business reason to do so. Any employee fraternizing with other employees outside of work in a non-company sponsored activity, regardless if they are with peers, subordinates, or supervisors, do set themselves up for entering an undesirable danger zone that is often impossible to overcome. I recommend you get a social life outside and away from work! The quick assessment below will give you some questions to assess the level of risk you are putting in your social activities with coworkers outside of work.

Quick Sabotage Assessment: Do I socialize inappropriately with my coworkers outside of work?

CAREER BUILDING CHARACTERISTICS	Y/N	CAREER SABOTAGING CHARACTERISTICS	Y/N
Do I organize a group baby shower for an expecting employee and invite everyone from the company, department, or branch?		*Do I pick only a few employees to invite, excluding one who works close but may not be invited? Do I invite only certain former employees, too?*	
Do I refuse to travel with coworkers, unless it is a conference or business reason to do so?		*Do I travel casually with my favorite boss or best friend, who happens to work with me? Do I take vacations or go camping together, just he/she and I?*	

(Quick Sabotage Assessment, Cont.)

CAREER BUILDING CHARACTERISTICS	Y/N	CAREER SABOTAGING CHARACTERISTICS	Y/N
Do I join all the coworkers from my department when we gather for an activity? Example, on the first Friday of every month, is the whole team invited to the local "Alive after Five," so everyone feels the team spirit at the outing?		*Do I gather only a select few of my coworkers because we've become closer and consistently hang out together and drink on weekends? Do I make others jealous at the office because they missed the invite? Do I share anything at the event that others back at the office aren't privy to?*	
Do I invite my entire department to go to lunch at the newest restaurant in town, and include my supervisor if I think they might want to attend?		*Do I invite the coworkers who are my buddies to lunch, knowing we really don't want some of the employees to join us? Do I intentionally exclude my supervisor? Do I gossip during this lunch about any person or situation I am frustrated with at work?*	
Do I invite everyone who worked on a project recently for dinner after work to celebrate?		*Were there a few team members I intentionally left off the invite? Will this event cause some team members to be offended who weren't invited? Do I reward every project of this magnitude differently, based on my favorite team members?*	

(Quick Sabotage Assessment, Cont.)

CAREER BUILDING CHARACTERISTICS	Y/N	CAREER SABOTAGING CHARACTERISTICS	Y/N
Do I avoid one-off meetings I'm invited to with previous employees to gossip about team members and avoid any potential misconception about meeting? Instead, will I invite a previous longtime coworker to the office for a potluck lunch so everyone can catch up?		*Do I prefer one-off meetings so I can talk about things not appropriate at the breakroom table for everyone to participate in? Do I share happenings from work that should not be shared?*	
When invited to an after-hours event that knowingly will have some naysayer staff attending, do I kindly refuse to attend and explain the professional reason why?		*Do I attend a barbecue organized by a disgruntled employee because I am curious what everyone's stories might be and I want the inside scoop?*	
Do I support the company over a former employee when they complain about their experience after they leave the company? Do I keep hearsay out of the conversation?		*Do I share what is going on in the company because I'm just as curious as they are, even though there is no business reason to do so? Do I engage with those who are not loyal supporters of the company with after-hours gatherings or texting comments?*	
Do I work with the Human Resource Department to organize a company-wide trip to a hockey event so everyone can participate, and no one will feel left out?		*Do I invite a few of my favorite peers to the hockey game, or "most" of the employees within my branch, knowing that some may not be as fun to take along or wish to partake in activities, such as drinking?*	

(Quick Sabotage Assessment, Cont.)

CAREER BUILDING CHARACTERISTICS	Y/N	CAREER SABOTAGING CHARACTERISTICS	Y/N
When I go on a walk daily during lunch to get some exercise with a coworker, do I invite others? Do I keep work out of the conversation?		*Do I only walk with certain people, excluding others in the department? Do I consistently talk about those at work or frustrations, sharing details that are none of my peer's business?*	

Let me first share some safe, social activities I've seen work well and continue to support strong employee interactions. There are also tricks to keep you out of hot water when it comes to socializing with current or previous coworkers. Notice, I included "previous" coworkers. These are just as important of a social relationship to protect as existing coworkers, as there are often tight threads that carry into your current work environment from social activities. Simply stated, ensure that any activity is inclusionary, meaning the *entire* department or logical related people in the group are invited. It could be that all peers with the same ranking are invited to participate, such as all sales people or all accounting staff. Invite all who worked on a specific project, or all supervisors along with their employees. This forces you to be inclusionary and prevent assumptions that you intentionally didn't want certain individuals included. Know that it is important that you build relationships with your coworkers—but if it is done by ignoring sensitivity and a lack of awareness of the effect on those who may be excluded, it is not worth the potential swarming beehive that is likely to form. Cliques are dangerous in any environment, especially in the workplace!

I do encourage employers to support specific team activities that create trust, getting to understand and know each other on a deeper level, and strengthening beneficial relationships with coworkers. These might be events where the entire group, such as an entire compliance department, is invited to an activity. It's not as important if each participant attends, but more so that they were given the opportunity and equal encouragement to participate, should they choose. The important component that is dangerous if it exists is the characteristic of being exclusionary. If you choose to exclude certain teammates for a night after work to have drinks, this can become very challenging and set you up to be misinterpreted. The best self-assessment question to ask is, "Is it logical that these individuals were not included on the invite list if everyone in the company or immediate site area knew who all was invited?" If you are trying to keep an event quiet among certain coworkers, it's likely not an inclusive activity and you will be entering a danger zone, unless you are planning a surprise party for someone.

Let me share some examples of healthy fraternizing in the workplace. My company holds an annual camping retreat where all employees are invited to attend. The weekend is full of team activities, challenge courses, and gender-specific sleeping quarters. Employees select their carpool teams and off we go. The activities at this event are carefully planned to prevent any risk of exclusion, discrimination, or inappropriate behavior. We are careful to keep it voluntary if you wish to attend, but also ensure everyone knows they are welcomed. We focus on providing staff the opportunity to meet people from different departments and site locations. It has been a successful event for many years, primarily because we include everyone in the invitation, leaving little room for suspicious favoritism or false assumptions about intentions. There is a great bond that happens around the campfire while eating s'mores. And no one who made the conscious decision to stay home should feel unsafe when the camping stories come back into the office on Monday morning, as they know they chose to not go and were invited. What is interesting is even at this event, those individuals that do "clique off" separately are even seen as somewhat of non-team players, confirming the very concept shared in this chapter. Staff do not care for any activity where the cliques are so strong they appear to have their own personal agendas or favoritism with certain individuals. Staff don't miss a thing and everyone notices when this happens.

Another activity our team enjoys in my specific office location is our payday lunch gatherings. Monthly, an employee will throw out a random restaurant and invite everyone in the same building to join if they wish for lunch outside the office. There's no pressure and it is an open invite. The group is large enough that specific discussions about anything during lunch that might shift to being inappropriate don't generally happen while at lunch, mostly because we also have a culture of no gossip or drama. It's simply a time to tell stories and connect, and it works. Again, it is unlikely that anyone at the office would look at these lunch events and accuse the company of playing favorites, worry about buddying up with someone that is destructive to them because of the lunch discussion, or become jealous if they weren't invited.

On occasion, one of our leaders will invite their entire team to dinner for an appreciation event, such as a barbecue or team-building exercise. This may be after a specific goal is met or a major project is finished. This type of fraternization does not typically cause harm if handled professionally. In fact, it is healthy and has many great benefits. I enjoy hosting a dinner for my executives on occasion to show appreciation, and I invite them all. If I were to pair off and only invite a couple of them, others on the team would feel unsafe. As a side note though, what is important is that each leader of the same level offer to do the same if their teams have similar accomplishments, or it will cause resentments from the other employees in the other departments. If Sam is the only VP that takes his team to dinner, for example, then other departments will have a negative assumption about their team lead not doing the same. These are things you should discuss in your team meetings among all your leaders to ensure you have consistency.

I have a steadfast rule that if I socialize with my employees outside of work, it is typically a group invite, carefully ensuring I am not excluding a certain individual or supervisor. Appropriate fraternizing with company employees is best served when the setting is safe, and the purpose of the event is to build relationships and connect, all while supporting the team working together and understanding each other. Team members do gain great value when they are able to get to know each other's passions and personal interests. However, if a pairing off with a select few from the team occurs, tension and jealousy builds instantly, along with the fear of a lack of acceptance, even if nothing about work was discussed and it was an innocent random opportunity to gather. My experience is that it is next to impossible, even with the best intentions and commitment to each other, to not talk about work, other employees, or one of your bosses while away from the office with coworkers. It's simply what you all have in common, so the discussion is naturally pulled that way. Even when a consensus is agreed upon about not bringing work into the conversation if you gather, it almost certainly lands there at some time. This is because you have that one common bond, and you share many hours together within that common bond.

The goals of "one voice" and always supporting the company mission do not go away in these settings. If the gathering is not supporting "one voice," my recommendation is to make the choice not to participate. Know that you can't control what employees do on their personal time, but you can control your participation in activities with your coworkers on your personal time.

There was a time many years ago when one of my employees joined my husband and I on a trip with their spouse to Las Vegas for the weekend. It was a disaster when we returned back to the office, because the fun stories she innocently shared about random vacation happenings created a new jealousy in the other team members, and also a distrust from my other employees that this employee had become my new favorite. That was so far from the truth, but it stuck in my other employees' minds forever. They quit sharing, and quit including her in conversations. I learned it is never a good idea to take one-off trips with your coworkers or employees. It's simply not worth the risk. Even with a simple drink after work, it's better to avoid the creation of a misinterpretation that some may make towards the motivations behind the gathering or unintentionally stepping into a pit you can't get out of. If I want to share a hobby, for example, such as teaching others to build a wreath in my craft room, I will find a way to invite everyone on the team, break the invite into smaller groups that make sense, or bring the hobby to work. You won't see me, as much as I want to sometimes, invite one coworker to dinner with their spouse, excluding all others. It is so important you understand how to avoid getting yourself stuck in inappropriate one-off activities. Find as many opportunities where if you invite one, you invite all. Even though not everyone will attend, invite them anyway. Hold an occasional lunch out, invite everyone to join the lunch hour walk, throw out an invite to everyone for a local baseball game, and invite the group if you are hosting a Christmas party or summer picnic. Once again, be careful not to invite only a few coworkers. This goes without saying for baby showers, weddings, graduations, concerts, camping, wine tours, or floating the river. Invite all and make it clear when it is completely optional. The opportunity for those who do join together leads to some nice laughter and sharing personal stories that can be carried back into the workplace without any negative repercussions if everyone was invited. And then pull out your courage and stand up for the company or anyone spoken less of if an inappropriate discussion rises to the surface at any of these group events, even if it is with your most trusted confidant and friend as your coworker.

Geography can also create unintentional barriers, but it can be overcome, such as remote employees who may not work in the same town. What's important here is to focus on intentions and the reality of the geographic separation. Let's say a group of team members work in the office and one works from home. It would be natural that the four who work close together in the office join together for some function during lunch, but be careful you do your best to include the remote employee where possible. Sometimes it is "out of sight, out of mind," and that is normal. It's also something the remote employee must accept by the nature of their situation and they should not become obsessed about pointing out when they were left out. They will be. I see this on occasion where an employee who has received the blessing of working from home complains too often and unfairly about their lack of inclusion, and they don't recognize the setup is their choice or simply the nature of the situation. An employer shouldn't feel like they have to go out of their way to include the remote employee at the same level as if they were working in the office, especially if it is the employee's choice, but the employer should make a good faith effort. If the remote employee wants to be more involved, they can always choose to work in the office, if that is an option.

In addition, if you are an employee of a small remote department or branch outside your company's normal trade area, be careful you don't make it your mission to point out every time you are left out. This can cause you to appear to be a whiner and demand unfair expectations in this area. You simply will be left out because of the separation with geography and the lack of presence locally to build the same relationship and onsite familiarity. Instead, enjoy the advantages of the remoteness and avoid being jealous of the situation. Again, employers should do what they can to help make the good faith effort, but know it will never be equal or perfect. If you are an employee feeling left out, the most important thing is to ask yourself, "What were their intentions?" If you don't feel they intentionally left you out or aren't giving you the remote attention you desire, find a way to accept it as part of the tradeoff for working remotely when it really doesn't make a difference and stay professional. Don't sabotage your career by being "that" person who never misses an opportunity to point out when you weren't "equal" in the offerings you received at the remote location. Being obsessed and overly critical of when you feel like the minority or attempting to make your employer feel like they can never do enough for you is not a good idea.

Don't fraternize with separated employees.

I would like to offer some further suggestions about appropriate behavior when connecting with terminated or separated employees from your organization. I would avoid staff gatherings with employees who have left the organization, unless you also have an "invite one, invite all" approach. That seldom happens in this situation. Ex-employees are always curious about how the company is doing, and you may even feel like you owe it to them to keep them updated. Previous employees are always interested in who is still in what positions, where the company is going, and what recent changes have occurred. Know that you may be tempted to share proprietary or confidential information with a separated employee inappropriately because they used to be one of you.

If you know an employee left disgruntled or was asked to leave, not of their own choice—or maybe you don't know why they separated from the company—it is simply never a good idea to fraternize with this employee outside of work going forward. Attending the barbecue organized by a group of selected separated employees, and a few current ones they feel they can trust, is a setup for disaster! I personally stumbled into one of these situations where an employee resigned, and I was invited to join the, "Everyone is getting together for a drink after work to celebrate this employee's next journey." What wasn't said was that not everyone was invited, and there were several former employees there, some whom I did not know. The conversation immediately turned to negativity about one of the executives. This immediately put me in an awkward and risky situation, as I refused to participate in this type of conversation. Even worse, I became privy to information about that executive that I could not remove from my knowledge. I didn't want to think of the executive in terms of what I heard, I had no idea how much of it was true, and it was temptation for disrespect and drama if I pursued my curiosity.

What is typical as I visit with employees who fall victim to these traps on occasion is their regret for attending. These events often turn into a negative justification session from those no longer employed as to why they left, and an attempt to negatively influence and manipulate the employees who are still employed. Some employees who leave or are terminated, even for good cause, will stay in a resentment mode and attempt to destroy the company or their former boss. If they are successful in planting the negative seed, it makes them feel supported in their decision when they chose to change employers or make a poor choice to leave. If they were terminated, they often unprofessionally share a completely different story than what really happened, because they don't wish to share their own mistakes or lack of performance with this group.

If you are known as the employee who wants in on the dirt of a certain employee's situation, especially if they were terminated, you are setting yourself up to share the reputation of someone who lacks support for the organization you work for. This will break down trust between you and your supervisor. You will be positioning yourself to often hearing from victims, and not hearing the full truth. I have received more fictitious stories shared that come out of these gatherings that can never be refuted because of protecting confidentiality as a human resource responsibility, and I have seen them be incredibly destructive and unfair as to how current employees view their current employer.

It's fascinating to me how there can be two employees that never really worked closely together, and maybe neither respected each other while in the workplace, yet when one leaves under less than perfect terms, they immediately join at the hip outside of work or friend each other online. If you do this, it truly hurts your career and reputation. It's difficult to escape the assumption that you are more loyal to those on the outside that weren't loyal to your company than the inside, and that you enjoy the gossip world and participate in it. I've seen these groups called everything from company "has-beens" to company "haters." Be careful about getting sucked into this, as it will likely put you in situations where you will feel the need to share updates on what goes on inside your company, and it could potentially be used against you later. In addition, the legal ramifications of breaking confidentiality or setting yourself up to be involved in a wrongful termination lawsuit should be enough to scare you off from this behavior if nothing else doesn't.

Know that not all separated employees are negative towards the company they have left. Many are forever grateful for the role the company played in their career and held healthy relationships with their coworkers. Some may have simply left because of personal reasons, such as becoming a new parent or moving out of the area. The best practice if you want to connect with some of your former coworkers who were a positive influence is to invite them to the office for lunch with the group. This is a safe and protected environment. This is even true of current coworkers who were moved to a different department. If the separated employee does not wish for this to happen, one should question why this is, and use extreme caution. I have learned to be very careful about attending any staff event where separated employees are attending, unless all were invited and the get together was publicly announced. Examples of this that would be appropriate are an alumni event to celebrate a company's major milestone, such as a 100-year anniversary. Be very careful about inserting yourself into potential situations where separated employees are selectively invited, as your curiosity will not win when it comes to building your brand and career, nor will your desire to be the known gatekeeper of new information that is irrelevant to the success of your company.

So, in summary, give extra attention to protecting yourself when you build your social activities outside of work. And NEVER use it as a time to bash others or share your problems with those in attendance. Don't embed your problem or your personal issues into someone else's brain when they have no reason to know. If you do, your problem will now irrelevantly affect how your coworkers might feel about someone else or the company. It's just not cool. The same is true of casual smoke breaks or walks during lunch with coworkers: Be careful and don't talk shop. I have seen employees create such an unsurmountable amount of distrust, simply by showing poor judgment while fraternizing with selected employees outside of work. My recommendation is to ensure you have a social life outside of work with healthy friends and family who are not coworkers. As admirable as the intentions are when two responsible coworkers get together and socialize outside of work, it is next to impossible not to have discussions about work that lead to gossip and confidential conversations.

11: Become the Best You That You Can Be

This chapter summarizes the previous ten chapters. If I could only leave one bit of advice, it is to commit to improving and changing what is needed in you to become a better leader and person. Just knowing, for example, that you are a certain personality type or you have a certain leadership style, is not enough to build a successful career.

Oftentimes, organizations go through the process of identifying what our natural personality traits are, such as DISC or Strengths Finder assessments, but then the team players don't take the necessary action to identify how they can use that information to make the necessary change to effectively use the less dominant features for the betterment of the team. You should have many times in your career when you need to make the mental commitment to change. That change might include how to communicate more effectively with your team, how to become more organized, or maybe it's how to improve your time management skills. Regardless of the specific change needed today, what is more important is that you recognize you will always need to be working on something that will make you a better you. It is what will lead you to become successful in the different phases throughout your career. This is not something to take lightly, and is a requirement, not only to feel fulfilled and satisfied with your career, but also reach a higher level of success than you can imagine today.

You must BECOME THE BEST YOU THAT YOU CAN BE. There will always be more you can learn, changes you need to adapt to, and different jobs you should try. The most important thing is you stay true to yourself and ask yourself daily, "Am I being the best me that I can be?" I wouldn't say that it takes blood, sweat, and tears—but I would suggest it takes *courage* to become better at being you. Courage is where it starts! If you don't have the courage to dig deep and agree to necessary change, the courage to try something new, and the courage to have uncomfortable conversations, you will be holding back what it takes to be the best YOU.

I've written about all three of the following components that can help you with change throughout the previous ten chapters, but let me briefly summarize the three big Cs of Courage.

Own the courage to change.

The courage to change is the hardest courage to stick with and conquer. I've heard it takes anywhere from 21 days to six months for a new habit to take hold and stick, and I believe it is closer to the latter. We all want change in everyone else but often find it difficult to change ourselves, myself included. If you were to ask your team how many things they wish would change in your organization, every person would have comments about something they wish would be different. Many will simply be a desired change that fits their personality type better. Others will include advice based on their experience in previous walks of life. Some will simply be the result of how their own mind and wisdom formulate solutions. This is truly what happens in life. We typically lean towards the more comfortable preference that everyone around us changes to behave like we think things should be done and suits our personality, and oftentimes we want others to change more than we do.

It's so easy to see what we think needs improvement in other people to be acceptable in our way of thinking and doing. And quite frankly, it's also not that difficult to see the change needed in us to be a more effective employee and leader. We know it. Think about this for a minute: Rarely does a supervisor who has our best interest at heart coach us through a recommendation to improve our career and contribution to the organization that we don't agree would be valuable to improve and change. We just choose to ignore it or believe that it doesn't really affect those around us as much as it does. It usually rises to the surface if someone has the courage to bring it to our attention. But why do we wait so often for someone to bring it to our attention first? For some, it is that moment when it becomes real. But what would happen if you followed your gut and made the known changes you *already know* are needed to be better at you before anyone brought it to your attention? This is often the golden ticket to your career if you can master taking action before your boss speaks up about it. We often fill our minds with procrastination promises to ourselves and others, excuses based on the other party's behavior, or accept our current less-than-effective behavior because we can get away with it.

Oftentimes, we treat those we love or who matter the most the worst. Why is that? Because we think we can get away with it and we have the confidence they will stick with us, regardless of the inadequacies. In the workplace, it happens at times, but may not be so forgiving. So I encourage you to start today. Make a list of the things you want to be better at or already know you need to improve in. Think of all your blind spots that others might be seeing in you that you haven't gone to work on yet. Find the courage to do whatever it takes to work on it.

I find it most effective if you reach out and find accountability partners and strong, healthy mentors, but that won't work unless you are fully committed to find your vulnerability and truly own your inadequacies. It doesn't matter what level you are at in your organization: CEOs have the same need for humility and mentors as any entry level employee. All are growing in their careers, some just have different responsibilities. Accountability will give you a tremendous boost in your career and you won't sabotage yourself along the way if you can take this seriously.

You must be committed to change for the right reason so it does not cause you resentment later. If you are only changing to save your job, such as showing up to work on time because your boss pointed your tardiness out, you may not change in a professional manner, and that will not help your career. If you don't recognize the negative effect on your personal brand and reputation by being consistently late, not to mention the lack of respect from your team, you will stay resentful and the change will be short-lived. You'll either find yourself leaving the organization because you don't like the "demanded" change, or you will shift to defense tactics that will only get you short-term results. It is critical when you identify a change to become a better you, you must think broadly about the "why" behind the change you need to make, not just the "what."

An example might be if you put in extra short-term effort to get your sales figures up in the next month by just doing the minimum your boss asked, and you don't find a way to appreciate and build new skills to become a more effective salesperson, you will likely experience only a temporary lift in your sales and weak permanent results. Another example on a personal level might be one where you are trying to lose weight simply for vanity's sake for an upcoming beach vacation, rather than for the purpose that it can extend your life and improve the quality of your health long term. When building your career, it's important that when you need to make a courageous change you know is going to be difficult, you ask yourself the broader why and look at it as how it will help you reach another step on your career ladder—don't do it simply to meet your boss's demands in the short term. Truly find a way to understand how it helps the organization, then go to work and do it.

Know that as you grow in your organization and move up the ladder, the change required often moves from tactical to more behavioral and managerial. In the beginning of my accounting career, the focus was on accurate reconciliations and presenting meaningful financial statements to the board of directors. As my career grew and I took on more supervisory responsibilities, it then became how I handled strategic discussions effectively and how I lead my team through big decisions. The latter was much more difficult, requiring continuous change, humility, and courage to improve to be a proficient leader, and it took great stamina and commitment at times to perfect.

Unfortunately, when given the opportunity, many employees and executives put pride and ego on a higher shelf than vulnerability and the desire to perfect their leadership and communication, and it hurts their career. I've seen this even when given the opportunity to have mentors who can help them through a needed change. This is often because they are focusing on what they don't like about the change or perception of others in the short term, rather than how it can help them become a more proficient leader long term. Be careful if you find yourself making statements such as, "That's just not me," or "I don't like to work that way."

If it's right for your company and you can see the benefit of it for the organization and team as a whole, find a way to say you will change to accommodate it. Then work on your vulnerability and the building of a strong accountability partner or mentor. After all, if it were easy, you would have already done it. Ask your trusted confidants to speak truth into how you can become a better leader, then listen with the goal to reach success.

Own the courage to try something new and perfect a new skill.

As you grow your career, you will always run into a new situation, process, team, or challenge. Instead of stepping back from it because you have never done it before, step into it quickly and exude confidence. Even if you are afraid you will fail in certain areas, step into action with creating the steps to be successful in your mind and lean on the confidence your superiors have expressed in you. Sometimes this needs to be done in a split second. Other times you have plenty of time to plan.

As I grew my career, there were responsibilities I agreed to take on that I knew nothing about, and I mean nothing. The butterflies started circling in my stomach with the thought of how I was going to master this new challenge. But remember, if it can be accomplished, someone has to figure it out, so why not *you*? And believe it or not, you always have a team of cheerleaders that want you to be successful. That team may include your boss, your audience, or your family and friends. You have a team that wants you to be successful, so think about them as you take the courage plunge.

When I started my position as the VP of Finance at Idahy FCU, my responsibilities included managing the Y2K conversion and testing all of our systems. Holy cow! I was so underqualified to take on this two-year project. But I made the commitment I would communicate when I had no clue where to go next, relied on the many resources I knew I could discover if I really wanted to, and then attacked it one system at a time.

There were times I had to memorize basic technology or system jargon just to have an intelligent conversation with a vendor, but I committed to it and followed through. There were times I had no idea what the purpose was of the system I was testing, so I had to leave my pride at the door and willingly ask dumb questions to learn the basics.

Here's what I found: If you can keep your ego and pride in check, the world around you loves to share their expertise with you, even if you are a few ranks above them in your organization. It provides a perfect opportunity to build a relationship of mutual respect. There was no one that I felt judgment from. Instead, it was quite the opposite: They gained respect for me because I was willing to pull from their expertise. But remember, I didn't fake it. I approached it as having the ability to work through this large project, using multiple sources of information and people, and proved it.

The *only* person who heard some of my feelings of insecurity was my boss, but he also heard my confidence to achieve the project successfully. It's important to keep both of these thoughts in the equation if you get scared, which is fear followed by confidence and courage. The minute you shy away from an opportunity because you aren't sure you are capable, you have lost, unless you add the dose of confidence that you will, in fact, learn, simply because you must.

I remember my first months as the President and CEO at my current job, walking into an exciting first-time, all-day staff retreat we had planned. It hit me that I am going to need to speak in front of my entire team, who are also assessing my ability to lead my organization. The judgment was naturally high, which is to be expected when you know you have a new CEO. I would likely feel the same. I knew I was going to need to lead the efforts and get the day started on the right track with energy and encouragement. It was the first time I had ever been required to get in front of that many people and speak. Gulp! So I set my mind on the fact that someone has to do this, and the team is looking for me to step into this as their confident leader, so I did. I also reminded myself that they are all likely glad they aren't the one that has to be up front, so they were cheering for me to be successful.

Although I'm sure some may have picked up my nervousness in the first few seconds, I believe I crushed it as I grabbed the courage and added some enthusiasm, knowing my audience was cheering me on. I did not let myself go to the space of, "I can't do this." To be successful in that moment, it wasn't a choice. Since then, I've been asked to step into television commercials and interviews, radio segments, and speak at large public events. Each time, it gets easier. And it takes new courage each time I step up to the microphone. Taking my fears one step at a time and just doing it works.

I've been presented with very difficult situations where it was simply my job as the leader to calm the storm, and brainstorm solutions that could have serious implications if done incorrectly. These have taken courage to muster through. But the role of the CEO is simply to lead the team through uncharted waters, not have the answers to everything. That takes courage. So find your courage each time a new challenge comes your way and use it. Be keenly aware of when you exhibit a weakness of not being able to accomplish something.

The best example of this that I have seen is of the once "amateur artist" Paige Weber, who designed the cover of my book. She set out a few years ago to truly become a known professional artist, and committed to drawing a piece of art every day for one year, referred to as the *365 Days of Art*. She's a quiet, humble friend who inspired many as she publicly shared each masterfully created piece of incredible art every day for 365 days. In this year, she moved to a different city, got married, and had many life changes, but her commitment was stellar and unwavering. Did she need to have a little courage to make this leap and public commitment? Yes! Did it lead to a successful career for her as an artist? That's a resounding yes! You can check out her *365 Days of Art* at http://paigeweber.blogspot.com/. Her work has become masterful and inspiring to many, and her business is growing as a result.

Own the courage to have difficult conversations.

It takes courage to place your being into difficult conversations. To intentionally be at the table when a difficult conversation needs to occur naturally increases anxiety, mostly because it increases the fear of conflict and separation. But as you do it more often, especially in trusted groups and teams, it does become easier. It never becomes easy, just easier, unless you are a natural jerk.

Two of my favorite books that speak to this are *Crucial Conversations* by Kerry Patterson, Joseph Grenny, Ron McMillan, and Al Switzler, and *The Five Dysfunctions of a Team*, by Patrick Lencioni. Both provide great insight and practical applications to master the courage of holding difficult conversations. You will grow in understanding, wisdom, and courage when you master the art of having difficult conversations.

You must learn how to have conversations about the differences of opinions and work through conflict. If this makes the butterflies dance like an airshow in your stomach, you must courageously practice and attack it. If you don't, you'll eventually make a substandard supervisor with little respect, because you'll shy away from communicating what your employees really need to know to grow. And you won't stand up for your own self. You may also be too shy to simply offer new ideas, something your company can benefit from. To advance in your career, you must find common ground and be willing to discuss constructive criticism, ideas, and differences professionally, without creating gossip and drama in the process. Conflict doesn't have to be the big bodacious disagreement: It's simply discussing different preferences and ways of work. A group of employees always contains individuals who grew up in different walks of life, and they will be different. Supervisors will always be handed a smorgasbord of talent and personalities. You must be able to work effectively through this, or you may be labelled as a self-serving hero, wimpy, or two-faced, and none of these lead to a healthy, productive employee, supervisor, or career.

I can recall those key moments in my career when courage was the primary differentiator in a situation that reaped great benefits, where I was the only one or one of only a few that was willing to take it on. There were moments of truth with a supervisor who was missing a large blind spot that was hurting the company. There were moments where my growth needs weren't being meant and I needed to process a mutually beneficial needs assessment with my boss. And sometimes it was simply finding the courage to say something positive about a situation when the whispering circle of my peers were demeaning the very hands that were putting money in their bank accounts each payday. It worked. So grab some courage and celebrate when you discover you have it in you.

ABOUT THE AUTHOR

Connie J. Miller is an Idaho native with over 25 years of executive level leadership experience, including over 10 years as a President/CEO of Icon Credit Union, a complex financial institution which ranks in the top 2% of healthiest credit unions in the nation. She is a public speaker and strong community leader, and her passions include building strong cultures in the workplace and mentoring employees to reach their maximum potential.

Connie was recently awarded the Idaho Business Review's *Idaho Icon Award*, which is a statewide recognition of business pioneers who champion their industry through professional creativity, innovation, and leadership. Recipients are recognized for their notable success and demonstration of strong leadership both within and outside of their chosen field. Connie has also been recognized as one of Idaho's *CEOs of Influence* for her leadership, integrity, values, competitiveness and innovation, financial performance, corporate leadership and board service, and commitment to diversity.

Connie is passionate about helping non-profits and serves on numerous boards and committees. She has received many prestigious awards, including the highest award in Girl Scouting, namely the *Thanks Badge,* for her exemplary service. She has proven that avoiding pivotal mistakes throughout your career pays off with great dividends and life experiences.

How to contact Connie directly:
Email: ConnieJMiller836@gmail.com
LinkedIn: Connie J. Miller

This Book is Proudly Published
By ZJN Media & Publishing
Meridian, Idaho

$19.95

ISBN 978-0-692-19556-7

51995>

9 780692 195567

Made in the USA
Monee, IL
15 October 2021

80025365R00100